ID700877

WILLING AND UNABLE

WILLING
AND
UNABLE

*Doctors' Constraints
in Abortion Care*

Lori Freedman

DISCARD

Vanderbilt University Press

NASHVILLE

362.19888
F853w

© 2010 by Vanderbilt University Press
Nashville, Tennessee 37235
All rights reserved
First Printing 2010

This book is printed on acid-free paper.
Manufactured in the United States of America

Book design and typesetting by Judy Gilats

Library of Congress Cataloging-in-Publication Data

Freedman, Lori, 1973–
Willing and unable : doctors' constraints in abortion
care / Lori Freedman.
      p. cm.
Includes bibliographical references and index.
ISBN 978-0-8265-1714-2 (cloth : alk. paper)
ISBN 978-0-8265-1715-9 (pbk. : alk. paper)
1. Abortion—United States—Prevention. 2. Reproduc-
tive rights—United States. 3. Hospitals—Medical staff—
Clinical privileges—United States. I. Title.
[DNLM: 1. Abortion, Legal—United States. 2. Health
Services Accessibility—United States. 3. Physicians—
United States. WQ 440 F853w 2010]
HQ767.5.U5.F745 2010
362.19'88802—dc22
2009041258

a/11

CONTENTS

PREFACE

Today, in the early twenty-first century in the United States, health policy-
makers, ethicists, and advocates are actively debating the rights of health
practitioners to deliver care according to their own consciences. The idea
that particularly troubles Americans is that physicians could be forced to
participate in abortion care (or other reproductive health care) when they
do not want to. In this book I show that, given the way abortion care is
marginalized in American medicine, and given that "conscience clauses"
extend to health-care institutions that regulate the practices of physician
employees, the problem is quite the opposite: physicians who want to provide abortions within mainstream American medicine often cannot. While
such clauses ensure that individuals have the right *not to* provide abortion
care, they ineffectively ensure that physicians have the right *to* provide
abortion care.

The inability of physicians to include abortion care in American mainstream medical practice is the main exploration of this book. Readers
predominantly interested in structural obstacles to abortion practice may
want to focus their attention on Chapters 2, 5, and 6. Chapter 2 looks at
the history of how abortion care exited mainstream medicine and how
abortion clinics came to provide 93 percent of abortions. Chapter 5 presents the multilevel barriers to abortion practice that physicians in this
study faced after residency. Chapter 6 examines abortion prohibitions in
Catholic-owned health-care institutions and their effects on the medical
practice of physicians in the study, especially during the management of
miscarriages.

There is a second important focus in this book, not reflected in the
title. Despite conventional wisdom, ideology and practice are not neatly

aligned in the context of abortion care. Sometimes "pro-choice" physicians have complicated feelings about providing abortions. Physicians' reasons for not providing abortions often extend beyond their fears of violence, stigma, and the professional consequences of involvement with abortion. At the same time, some physicians who oppose abortion find themselves more sympathetic to the need for abortion after they are exposed to that need during their residencies. Chapters 3 and 4 tell the moral and emotional stories of physicians' choices around abortion care. These chapters tease apart how particular training experiences and interactions with patients shape doctors' orientations toward abortion care in ways they did not necessarily expect.

It has been some time since social scientists regarded Western medicine as an objective, depoliticized science. While physicians may share a certain set of skills and knowledge from their professional training, physician practice is subject to diverse financial and political tensions in addition to individual preferences. Nevertheless, abortion politics often extend their reach into surprising corners of the physician experience, shedding light on individual and institutional ideas about women's sexual behavior, with real consequences for women's reproductive lives.

ACKNOWLEDGMENTS

I can start nowhere else but with a heartfelt thank-you to my mentor Carole Joffe. Her support over the past decade has been steadfast and essential. Carole is an inspirational model for engaged academia, never losing sight of the bigger picture and its constituents. I am grateful to Drew Halfmann for his incisive feedback and masterful way of helping me understand what I was trying to say (and then saying it back more beautifully). Sharon Kaufman has been a burst of intellectual stimulation for me, offering new theoretical challenges, exciting reframing of ideas, and (when most critical) deadlines! Liz Roberts, my friend and most informal mentor, has been enormously influential at pivotal moments, elucidating aspects of power that helped me place my analyses in a broader historical and cultural context. I thank Danielle Bessett, Kira Foster, Tracy Weitz, an anonymous Vanderbilt reviewer, and all of my amazing colleagues at ANSIRH and the Bixby Center for Global Reproductive Health here at the University of California, San Francisco, for helping me refine my thinking on this book in its later stages.

I am most deeply indebted to Jody Steinauer, Uta Landy, and Phil Darney for identifying the need for this research and then supporting me in multiple ways to undertake it. This research was generously supported by the Kenneth J. Ryan Program, the Mary and Lloyd Schwall Fellowship at UC Davis, and a block grant from the Department of Sociology at UC Davis. And it could not have happened without the kindness of the four unnamed residency programs, their directors and administrators who helped connect me with graduates from their programs, and, of course, the physicians themselves whom I interviewed for this research. Also of critical importance were Cynthia Harper, Joe Speidel, Jody Steinauer, and

Tracy Weitz, who made it possible for me to finish the book in a timely manner through my visiting scholarship at the Bixby Center for Global Reproductive Health at UCSF. Thank you to Michael Ames at Vanderbilt University Press for his interest and confidence in the book project, and to copy editor Jessie Dolch, managing editor Ed Huddleston, and indexer Alexa Selph for contributing their talents and their extraordinary attention to detail.

I also thank Vicki Smith, Lyn Lofland, Laura Grindstaff, Fred Block, Jim Cramer, Ming-cheng Lo, Patrick Carroll, and Deborah Paterniti from the Department of Sociology at UC Davis for their meaningful contributions to my intellectual development—as well as Kristin Luker at Berkeley for an unforgettable yearlong seminar on morality. I thank Bimla Schwarz, Debbie Bamberger, Rebecca Jackson, and Alisa Goldberg for giving me my start and patiently educating me in technical aspects of reproductive health care and research. I am grateful to members of my writing group—Julie Collins, Joan Meyers, Magdalena Vanya, Jennifer Gregson, Macky Yamaguchi, Alie Alkon, Dina Biscotti, Jaime Becker, and Julie Setele—for providing excellent conditions for productivity, fun, and intellectual growth. I am also grateful to Joe Eisenberg and Sue Wilson for lending me their critical minds on many a needed occasion in addition to their outstanding companionship.

Thank you to several close friends who have helped me talk this book through (while running, cooking, watching children, etc.) over the past few years: Deborah Barron, Kate Delaplane, Steve Feierabend, Amy Gordon, Debra Hill, Jennifer Mangel, Emily Merideth, Robert Ratner, Jen Schradie, Jennifer Tuveson, Tanya Williams, Anna Wong, and, especially, Kristina Ryan, who has probably logged the most hours helping me make sense of it all. I am eternally grateful to my midwives, Cindy Haag and Griselda Hernandez, for helping me get my babies out! (Definitely harder than the book.) And with those babies came a huge network of supporters, especially caregivers, preschool communities, and teachers, who have all brought much needed wisdom and confidence to this child-rearing endeavor.

I am grateful to my mother, Judy Freedman, for the loving child care and endless commitment to my academic success, up to the last printout. Thanks to Bill Skoonberg for his helpfulness in every way and to my sister, Lisa Freedman, for understanding me. Thank you to my father, Jonah Freedman, for the visits and garden support, and for just listening. Thank you to my grandparents, Lil and Leo Simon and Sol and Violet Freedman, for their faith and support from day one. And many thanks to Chandra-jyoti Wildfire and Ziv Tzvieli for all of the love they show the kids and for providing a much needed safety net at crunch times.

Of course, the biggest thank-you of all goes to Ori Tzvieli. I feel enormously blessed to have such a compassionate and loving husband, friend, and co-parent. That he is also a talented and willing editor is a tremendous gift. Thank you for tolerating the late-hour desperate pleas to read drafts and for providing me with feedback I respect and trust. Finally, I dedicate this project to my two girls, Hannah and Ruby, my two bright shining lights. Your smiles and deliciousness fill my days with joy and sustain me. May the world, your world, only become a better place.

WILLING AND UNABLE

CHAPTER 1

Introduction

That was probably the most disappointing thing about training residents. You know, for what? *To do nothing?* I mean, they obviously would
refer [their abortion] patients, and they would take good care of their patients, both pre- and post-care. But, you know, it was disappointing to not
have them *have the guts* to stand up and say, "I'm going to do it."

DR. DAVIS CHASEY, *retired founder and director of a residency abortion clinic*

Dr. Chasey's disappointment that his resident physicians of obstetrics and
gynecology didn't "have the guts" to perform abortions after graduating
was harsh, yet poignant.[1] Here sat a man, nearly eighty years of age, explaining how he had dedicated his career to providing abortion to women
in a conservative state and how he had advocated to keep his clinic open
under unsupportive conditions, at times facing hostility from colleagues,
so that he could continue to train the next generation of abortion providers. And yet, very few of Dr. Chasey's trainees performed abortions
after graduating from residency. Indeed, during Dr. Chasey's career, he
saw the number of abortion providers begin a national decline in the early
1990s, most significantly in politically conservative and rural areas, making abortion less accessible for some of the most economically disadvan-
taged women in the United States. Dr. Chasey saw abortion training as
a career calling, a way to prevent abortion-related deaths and hospital-
izations such as those he had witnessed before abortion was legalized in
1973 by the Supreme Court decision in *Roe v. Wade*.[2] Remembering experiences from his own training in the 1950s, he recounted: "When I was in

[obstetrics and gynecology, ob-gyn] residency training we had a ward of about twenty beds, which was full all the time with women having 'miscarriages.' And we suspected that these were not all spontaneous abortions, but we had no way of proving it. If you asked a woman, she would obviously deny it. And those women had problems. They had excessive bleeding. They had infections, sometimes bad infections . . . After *Roe v. Wade* . . . those wards closed. There was nobody to put on them." Before *Roe*, Dr. Chasey had discreetly performed abortions for his patients when asked. "They were infrequent but I did them," he said. "And I just felt very strongly that women had this right." In the early 1970s Dr. Chasey took a faculty position at a medical school in the Midwest where he was asked to set up the school's first abortion service. He started it from the ground up and worked there for nearly thirty years until his retirement, after which the clinic promptly closed.

Seven of the physicians I interviewed were trained by Dr. Chasey. They all spoke fondly of him; they were compelled by his story, his politics, and his genuine concern for his patients. After they learned how to perform abortions in his residency clinic, many of them continued to moonlight during residency at a remote abortion clinic. Most expressed appreciation for the skills they gained during abortion training. They frequently used the word "important" to describe abortion training. One physician said, "I was happy that I was learning how to do something that I thought was important." Another said, "I thought it was important . . . it should be done in a safe, comfortable environment." Still another, referring to her patients, said, "To do abortion the right way in the right setting is very important to the quality of their life." Yet, while their feelings about the importance of abortion care did not change after residency, only one of them still included elective pregnancy terminations in her practice at the time of the interview (for abortion terminology, see Appendix A).[3]

This book examines how the politics of abortion have shaped its practice in the United States. In essence, I ask, What happened to Dr. Chasey's residents after he trained them in abortion care? Was it simply "guts" that they lacked? Such a notion implies that the problem lies with the individual failings of the residents. If this were true, how could we measure the courage required to perform abortions as a newly graduated physician starting out in practice in the 1970s compared with today? Have doctors changed so much? Or is it the social and medical context of reproductive health care that has changed significantly?

Abortion is a common and safe medical procedure technically similar to that performed during a miscarriage. It is easily learned by obstetrician-gynecologists (ob-gyns), general practitioners, and surgeons and can be done in physician offices (during the first trimester of pregnancy). In 2005, abortion was the third most frequently performed surgery on women of reproductive age (age fifteen to forty-four), following behind two birth-related procedures: cesarean section (C-section) and obstetrical laceration repair.[4] Yet despite abortion's commonness, it has become highly marginalized within medicine such that very few physicians provide abortions.

Abortion may be technically simple, but integrating it into one's medical practice is not. The near-total segregation of abortion into freestanding clinics and the constant legislative battles over the details of abortion care have presented formidable challenges. Furthermore, reimbursement rates have not risen with inflation over the past three decades, making the financial incentive of abortion a product of medicine's past (Rose 2007). More extreme in its effect, however, has been the rise of a powerful anti-abortion movement, members of which have regularly threatened and occasionally murdered abortion providers. Combine all of these issues with the escalation of political combat between social conservatives and liberals over abortion, and physicians undoubtedly have many reasons to be deterred from abortion care.

To encourage new physicians to provide abortions, reproductive health advocates have focused a great deal of effort on educating and politicizing medical students and residents. Some advocates attribute the waning number of abortion providers in the United States to the historical ignorance of younger physicians; that is, unlike Dr. Chasey, younger physicians typically have not seen firsthand the horrors of what women went through before abortion was legalized. They argue that if residents and medical students were better educated about this history, they would step up to the challenges of providing abortion just as their graying predecessors did. Such thinking has fueled successful organizations such as Medical Students for Choice, which has proliferated in medical schools throughout the United States since the first chapter was founded in 1994.

The organization was created to bring abortion into the medical school curriculum as well as to inspire and support the next generation of abortion providers. Indeed, research supports the link between the strength of physician beliefs around abortion and the likelihood of physicians providing abortions after residency (Steinauer et al. 2008). Yet despite increased medical student activism and residency abortion training, only half of the physicians who intend to include abortion in their practices end up doing so after graduating residency (Steinauer et al. 2008). Clearly, both abortion training and support for abortion rights are necessary preconditions for abortion practice, but they alone are insufficient.

Ultimately, there are both *willing* and *unwilling* physicians. The physicians willing to provide abortions, despite multiple disincentives, are the primary focus of this book. However, all of their willingness is embedded in a medical structure that makes abortion provision unlikely, if not impossible. Because of this, I distinguish those who are *willing and able* from those who are *willing and unable* and argue that the distinctions between the two groups derive more from structural constraints than from individual strengths and weaknesses. While physicians may need "guts" or bravery to provide abortion in the face of abortion stigma and violence, I argue that it is rarely enough for them to overcome additional barriers presented by major changes in the organization of medicine: That is, since the 1980s, the locus of power has shifted away from individual physicians and into the hands of their managers, employers, and insurers, who may have conflicting preferences and policies about abortion and are able to constrain, if not prohibit, its practice. *Thus, many physicians cannot provide abortions within their medical practices even if they want to.* In contrast to the British nationalized health-care system, for example, which includes abortion within its services, the responsibility for providing abortion in the U.S. market-driven system has become increasingly consolidated within freestanding abortion clinics beleaguered by antiabortion harassment and legislation. At the same time, advocacy efforts to reverse the trend by encouraging physicians to integrate the procedure into their general practices have had limited success.

Study Methods

In 2006, I set out to answer the question of why doctors with abortion training discontinue the practice post-residency. I interviewed graduates from four ob-gyn residency programs around the United States chosen for their geographic diversity (Midwest, South, Northeast, and West) and their longstanding inclusion of abortion training in their core curriculums. In all, approximately 150 physicians who had graduated in the years 1996–2001 received a letter requesting their participation in a study examining their experiences with abortion in training and in practice. It was forwarded to them by their former residency directors, who included a letter asking them to participate in an in-depth interview with me— which I imagine was more influential than the gift certificates I offered. In this way, my access to physicians was paved by the support of those who have both power and investment in the training of ob-gyns. Such support made my experience of "studying up" much easier than it might have been otherwise (Nader 1969).[5]

Abortion training has been routine for many years in the four selected programs, and residents must *opt out* if they do not want to participate. More often, in this country abortion training is done the other way around: residents have to *opt in* if they want to participate during their elective (free-choice) rotation time. I did not include elective-only programs because I assumed that those who opt in would be more highly politicized around abortion—given that there are many important competing elective choices—than are residents who train because it is a routine component of their program. I wanted to minimize highly politicized residents as a portion of my sample because a sample of such graduates might yield a disproportionate number of abortion providers, who I already knew were a rare breed. Rather, I wanted to speak with the individuals who primarily identify as ob-gyns (not abortion providers) to get a better sense of how and why abortion often gets excised from their ob-gyn practices.

By recruiting from opt-out programs, I could also speak with a significant number of amenable or *willing* physicians, whom I characterize as not necessarily centrally identifying with abortion as an ideological cause or professional obligation, but not morally opposed to performing abortions. Many physicians from routine training programs would not seek out abortion training if it were not part of the core curriculum. As one southern residency faculty member explained: "[Abortion training] was not a reason for someone to either choose [the program] or not choose it . . . it just wasn't focused on. Perhaps people might be more apt to choose it because of the . . . abortion training, but there are also going to be perhaps an equal number of people that would still come here regardless . . . because they liked the other aspects of the program and it was stronger and they wanted to stay in the South." Opt-out programs also provided the benefit of minimizing social stigma around abortion provision. If training in abortion was expected along with training in all other ob-gyn procedures, abortion would be as normalized as is possible in our current political and medical context. It follows, then, that the residents I spoke with trained under optimal conditions to foster the view of abortion as an acceptable and important part of an ob-gyn practice.

Forty of the 150 physicians returned consent forms in the mail, and of those, I interviewed 30 individuals—22 women and 8 men in cities of various sizes (see Appendix B). I visited all four residency programs and interviewed physicians—half over the phone and half in person—in their homes, hospitals, and offices. One particularly talkative physician gave most of his interview over the phone from his car. Another allowed me to interview her in her clinic office during a tight lunch break while she simultaneously ate and pumped her breast milk. (I had only recently weaned my own child, so it seemed to both of us a naturally efficient use of time.) Regardless of the circumstances, physicians generally shared quite freely in the interviews. My social location undoubtedly helped in putting the physicians at ease. Respondents' ages ranged from the mid-thirties to the early forties, and I was thirty-two at the time—both young enough for physicians to still perceive me as an unthreatening and eager listener and old enough for them to generally assume that I could relate to their life experiences. I also interact regularly with physicians in familial, social, and professional contexts, lending me a high degree of familiarity with physician culture. Finally, I understand a great deal of "medicalese" related to obstetrics and gynecology based on my previous research experiences in an abortion clinic, on a labor and delivery ward, and in a family planning clinic, as well as (perhaps most importantly) my own experience giving birth twice.

I also conducted ten supplementary interviews with residency directors, fellows, and administrators in connection with the programs; most of
these interviews happened during visits to residency sites. The two interview groups (graduate and supplementary) break out quite differently in
my mind. Of the original sample of thirty graduates that I pursued, twenty-
eight had no specific focus on abortion in their practices; they were "your
average" ob-gyns or subspecialists, and, as I had expected, most were not
highly politicized. To be sure, when pinned down, they were largely pro-
choice,[6] because of the self-selecting nature of the study, and some had
become more supportive of abortion rights after their experiences in residency. Still, this was not a primary source of identification for most graduates I interviewed. In contrast, the supplementary group included individuals who had specifically dedicated much of their careers to abortion provision, training, or both; therefore, they were relatively more focused on
abortion politics and reproductive rights. Together, they provided a fuller
picture of the physician experience vis-à-vis abortion, as well as a useful
comparison of personal and professional perspectives and priorities.

I do not view the fact that most of the individuals in my sample were
socially liberal in their sentiments about abortion as a limitation to the
study. My research questions were more focused on constraints on abortion care for those physicians who would be willing to provide it than for
those who would not. The physicians I sought out had already settled at
least some of their ontological debates and knew their moral boundaries
around abortion care, given that most had performed numerous abortions during training. The scope of our discussions included physicians'
personal moralities about abortion; however, the interviews focused more
on how abortion practice was prohibited or tolerated in their new professional lives. While four interviews I conducted with physicians who opted
out of performing abortions during residency provided insights into their
moral discomfort with abortion, I primarily wanted to find out what keeps
physicians who feel positive about providing abortion from doing so.

Abortion Politics and Abortion Work

Much of the social science literature about abortion has emphasized its
political dimensions in the broadest context. In particular, scholars such

as Rosalind Petchesky, Kristin Luker, Carole Joffe, and Faye Ginsburg writing in the 1980s elucidated the ways in which the politics of abortion extend far beyond the debate about how to define the fetus. Abortion is also the site of a larger debate about gender. The very right of a woman to terminate a pregnancy that she does not want, without seeking permission from a spouse, parents, or any authority but her own, has become a symbol of many tensions surrounding the changing roles of men and women in society. Americans (physicians included) are generally more supportive of abortion when women's hardship is pronounced (rape, incest, severe poverty) and less so when women terminate pregnancies for reasons they deem "selfish" (education or career, wrong partner, child spacing), supporting the notion that fetal death is not the most offensive aspect of abortion for many Americans. Rather, the most offensive issue may be the notion that women can shirk the mother role. Deeply embedded in American society is the belief that women who have sex implicitly become obligated toward parenthood more so than men. Extricating oneself from unintended pregnancy is thus a gendered experience, both physically and socially.

Since these analyses of abortion politics in the 1980s, the conflict over abortion has remained animated by the same fundamental concerns; however, the scope of activism has expanded. In the 2000s, abortion politics have become firmly lodged within policy battles related to sex education, public funding of "crisis pregnancy centers," and, most notably, contraception (Fields 2008; Joffe 2010; Luker 2006). The religious right has come to consider abortion to be the tip of the iceberg. The movement is interested in multiple points of intervention into the lives of individuals and families in order to address perceived threats to the traditional family structure, especially out-of-wedlock sexual activity and procreation.

My work speaks to a smaller, yet crucial body of scholarship that has focused on the relationship of abortion to mainstream medicine (Halfmann 2003; Imber 1986; Jaffe, Lindheim, and Lee 1981; Joffe 1986; Joffe 1995; Mohr 1978; Reagan 1997; Simonds 1996). This literature examines how abortion politics (broadly speaking) and stigma have shaped abortion care, medical policy, and the physician experience over the past 150 years. I also locate this research within a growing bioethics and sociology of morality literature concerned with how professionals understand right and wrong in their work (Abbott 1983; Anspach 1993; Bosk 1979; Bosk 1992; Casper 1998; Curlin et al. 2007; Dickens 2008; Lynch 2008; Rapp 1999; Zussman 1992). Scholarship within this tradition documents and analyzes how professionals negotiate morally uncharted terrain, how they daily make meaning of contested aspects of their work, and how they interpret their professional obligations to their patients and society. Physicians' experiences and understandings of their professional obligations are integral to the study of women's reproductive rights because, at this point in time, members of the medical profession remain uniquely capable of ensuring those rights.[7] Women's access to safe abortion care is first and foremost circumscribed by physicians' willingness and ability to provide it.

The Changing Nature of Medical Authority

Physicians are critical protagonists in U.S. abortion history. Because medical authority has so readily translated into *moral authority* in American culture, physicians have done more than perform abortion procedures: they have been powerful figures in shaping understandings of female sexuality and in sanctioning policy change regarding abortion. This is because physicians also possess *cultural authority*, which is a broader way to think about how medicine conveys moral messages. By virtue of the expertise of professionals, their authority "extends to the meaning of things" (Starr 1982: 13). Medical professionals impart definitions of reality through their clinical interactions with patients on the individual level as well as through political lobbying on the institutional level. Physicians attained a tremendous degree of cultural authority during the rise of their profession in the twentieth century, in large part because of the unprecedented successes of science in healing. Over the past century, science and the pursuit of health have displaced religion as a guiding force in the daily lives of many Americans (Foucault 1978; Parsons 1951; Rose 2001).[8]

Physicians have relied on their moral authority to designate the rightness or wrongness of things, much as religious figures have historically done. During the ascendance of the American medical profession, medical leaders employed this moral authority to actively develop prevalent tensions around female sexuality and fetal personhood with significant consequences for women's lives (Luker 1984). For example, in nineteenth-century America, abortion was not only legal before "quickening" (the onset of the sensation of fetal movement, at about five months), it was more visible than it is now. Numerous ads for "periodical pills" and "professional services" posted by a variety of health practitioners in nineteenth-century newspapers and magazines offered to cure female "problems" and menstrual "irregularity" (Mohr 1978; Reagan 1997).[9] Abortion became more problematic in the late nineteenth century when the newly founded American Medical Association (AMA) undertook an effort, which historian James Mohr (1978) termed "the physicians' crusade," to discredit and supplant competing health practitioners without mainstream medical training, such as homeopaths and midwives, by focusing on their involvement with abortion. The overt purpose of the physicians' crusade was to educate people about the existence of fetal life before quickening. Much as antiabortion protesters would do nearly one hundred years later, late-nineteenth-century physicians displayed pictures of embryos to visually impart the "humanness" of aborted fetal or embryonic life. Thus, abortion was not always as controversial and stigmatized as it is today, but the professionalization project of American medicine contributed greatly to making it so.

Physicians also sought to correct the presumed immorality of women who neglected "marital duties" in their desire not to reproduce (Smith-Rosenberg 1986). Their concern had a eugenic component, namely, racist fears held by ruling-class whites (which included physicians) of becoming outpopulated by immigrants, such as Italian and Jewish immigrants, who were not perceived as being white at the time (Petchesky 1990).

The AMA's campaign to criminalize abortion accomplished several things beyond making the practice illegal. It took abortion out of the private realm, making it a public problem. By positioning physicians as morally and scientifically informed vis-à-vis pregnant women, this campaign legitimized physicians as moral authorities about female sexuality and reproduction. It put them on the side of the law, further delegitimizing the competing health practitioners they wished to displace. And finally, it strengthened the budding medical profession by increasing the health territory under its purview.

Advocating antiabortion policies in state legislatures was one fruitful way for physicians to attain legitimacy and professional dominance. While they had no better healing abilities than competing health practitioners at that time, they did have higher social status and greater access to the political system. Ultimately, physicians were instrumental in changing abortion law, but enforcement was slow to follow. Abortion was still widely available through midwives and "discreet" physicians for several decades. At this time, physician associations conducted quiet internal investigations of physicians performing illegal abortions, giving professional reprimands rather than turning physicians over to the state for punishment. Historically, the American medical profession has maintained autonomy by positioning itself as capable of self-policing in matters of medical mistakes and physician substance abuse, among other transgressions (Bosk 1979; Freidson 1970; Starr 1982). Self-regulation is a defining characteristic of professions, and the medical profession maintained more autonomy than most in this regard. Control was thus held tightly by the AMA, which had been gaining national strength and power during the early twentieth century.

While cracking down on abortion patients or doctors was relatively uncommon, between 1890 and 1920 midwives were publicly portrayed by physicians, public health workers, and reformers as unsafe health practitioners, and members of the medical profession strongly supported their prosecution. Physicians had already taken an interest in controlling the birth practices of midwives as part of their larger effort to broaden their professional domain. After the turn of the twentieth century, they were able to assume control of not only birth, but also the few abortions that were still legal based on maternal health conditions. Thus, physicians gained the medical authority (as opposed to that of other practitioners) and the moral authority (as opposed to that of the pregnant woman herself) to determine which abortions were justified and which were not.

In the 1920s and 1930s, abortion rates rose because of economic pressure and women's increased need to find and keep work (pregnant women were routinely fired from their jobs) and to control family size. Physicians who were providing illegal abortions during the Depression era were relatively visible and widely tolerated by police. Tolerance of illegal abortion by physicians in the early twentieth century was possible in part because of the mounting authority of the profession, but also because, as historian

Leslie Reagan (1997) argues, during certain historical periods there has been greater social acceptance of abortion as a necessity. In the 1940s and 1950s, however, the law stopped looking the other way, and medical advances such as penicillin allowed women hospitalized for life-threatening complications to survive to testify against abortion providers; before antibiotics women frequently died from infection when abortions went bad.

Raids and prosecution of these established illegal abortion providers deterred new physicians from providing illegal abortion care, making safe abortion less available. Concurrently, and contributing to decreasing access to safe abortion, hospitals began to set up therapeutic abortion committees to more closely screen women who wanted legal abortions. For the three decades preceding legalization, pregnant women with financial resources pleaded their cases to professionals for relatively rare abortion slots in the hospital. In 1969 only thirteen thousand legal abortions were reported in the United States (Lindheim 1979), while the number of illegal abortions at that time was estimated to be as high as 1.2 million (Joffe 1995: 211). Deaths from illegal abortions are difficult to estimate and the rates given by multiple studies in the twentieth century vary widely, in part because of the politics driving such studies and in part because of the lack of clear data, given that the stigma surrounding abortion may have led physicians to document deaths as related to miscarriage or infection, among other things. For example, while 320 abortion-related deaths were officially calculated by coroners in 1961 in the United States (Tietze 1980: 95), three credible sources from the 1960s estimated a minimum of 5,000 such deaths per year in this country (Kummer and Leavy 1966; Lader 1966; Schwarz 1968). Whatever the actual numbers, one thing has been clear: maternal mortality drastically declined after abortion was legalized in 1973. That year, data from the Centers for Disease Control (CDC; now the Centers for Disease Control and Prevention) revealed only nineteen abortion-related deaths in the United States; from 1990 to 2000, between four and eleven women died from abortion-related causes each year (Strauss et al. 2004).

Most of the abortion-related deaths before legalization were due to self-induced abortion when women tried to disrupt their own pregnancies by inserting objects into the cervix, often resulting in infection or excessive blood loss. According to Reagan (1997), this fact indicates that the "back-alley butcher" was more a rarity exploited by the media than a phenomenon of real prevalence. The image, however, of a nonphysician "quack" hurting desperate women is one that has historically held great purchase in the American imagination and further bolstered the medical authority of credentialed physicians.

Above ground, physicians were involved with changing abortion law through physician advocacy groups such as the Association for the Study of Abortion (originally called the Association for Humane Abortion), founded by influential ob-gyn Alan Guttmacher in 1965. Many physicians supported legal changes advocated by the American Law Institute to permit abortion for mental or physical health reasons, for fetal abnormalities, and in cases of rape and incest (Joffe 1995). Still others joined the broader multiprofession movement to repeal all existing abortion laws (the National Association for Repeal of Abortion Laws, NARAL).

During conventions, in journal editorials, and through advocacy work, physicians debated the concern over becoming "mere technicians" under the NARAL model that would permit "abortion on demand" (Joffe 1995: 47). Physicians' claims of professionalism and authority have historically rested precisely on their exclusive health knowledge and role as diagnosticians. The idea that the pregnant woman can "diagnose" her own necessity for the procedure represented a way of de-skilling physicians as diagnosticians. In the early 1970s, physicians were still at their height of power and autonomy, and a burgeoning medical ethics movement had only begun to critique abuses of that power. Therefore, physicians actively struggled with the idea that the patient should decide the problem and the course of treatment. A statement by one hundred ob-gyns urged the medical community to prepare to meet abortion needs should laws change and at the same time acknowledged, "For the first time, except perhaps for cosmetic surgery, doctors will be expected to do an operation simply because the patient asks that it be done" (AJOG 1972). Ironically, although *Roe* legally located abortion rights under the authority of the physician, in practice, legalization meant that physicians would largely relinquish their role in the decision-making process around abortion, and the moral authority would become that of the pregnant woman herself. This is a change that some physicians embraced, while others did not.

New Forces Shaping the Physician Experience

Several critical things happened simultaneously to shape the nature of physician authority at this juncture in the 1970s. Of course with *Roe*, physicians gained the legal power to do abortions at their own discretion; however, religious conservatives, who were shocked by the ruling, animated and expanded the antiabortion movement, bringing politics into doctors' offices like never before. At the same time, physicians began to experience a significant decline in autonomy because of two major forces that were gaining momentum: the medical ethics movement and managed care (Zussman 1992).[10] Both forces had emerged in order to control abuses of physician power increasingly documented in academic and popular venues during the 1960s and 1970s (Freidson 1970; Hafferty and Light 1995; Haug 1976; Ruzek 1978; Starr 1982).

Understanding the confluence of these forces on medicine is critical to understanding the difference between Dr. Chasey's medical world when he graduated residency and that of the physicians he trained thirty years later. Between the 1970s and 1990s the medical ethics movement (including the women's health and patients' rights movements) made major strides in reallocating power within medicine to patients through informed consent requirements and increased use of malpractice law; to institutional review boards through their oversight of research on human subjects; and to ethics committees in hospitals that approved and reviewed physician decision making (Rothman 1991). During this same time corporate bodies, rather than individual physicians, began to manage health-care delivery and to suppress reimbursement rates in order to control soaring medical costs. This financial restructuring resulted in major changes in the physician experience: decreased income, reduction in time per patient visit, and decreased autonomy over how to test or treat patients. Thus, in multiple ways, the medical profession became less sovereign and physicians themselves were to some extent dethroned.

The physician experience of abortion care was also drastically altered by the 1980s and 1990s. No longer was the decision between a pregnant patient and her doctor, as it had been envisioned in *Roe*. Instead, it became a decision involving several powerful entities, including the physician's employer, the physician's malpractice insurer, the physician's hospital or surgery center administrators, activists on both sides, and law-makers busy creating both protective and obstructive regulations around abortion. Many of these factors have contributed to a systemic squeezing of abortion services and personnel to the periphery of medicine.

While the "golden age of doctoring" may be over (McKinlay and Mar-ceau 2002), physicians today nonetheless maintain a significant degree of cultural and moral authority (Pescosolido, Tuch, and Martin 2001). This is true primarily because patients still depend on their medical expertise and physician associations still control most aspects of physician training and credentialing (Freidson 1984; 1994); that is, they still control membership to the club, but they no longer manage the club. To be sure, physicians col-lectively take on their managers—corporations and the government—over many issues, and abortion is occasionally one of them. But medicine has changed, and so must our understanding of the constraints with which physicians contend. Health maintenance organizations (HMOs), hospital administrations, insurance companies, and group practice owners restrict mainstream physicians' choices regarding abortion practice in multiple ways. As a result, willing physicians discussed in this book demonstrate that those wanting to include abortion in their practices often have an unsatisfying choice to make: either practice obstetrics and gynecology *or* provide abortions, but not both.

Not only have the conditions of medical practice changed, but physi-cian demographics are also different. In particular, physicians are increas-ingly female. In 2006 when this research was completed, women consti-tuted nearly one-third of the physician workforce in the United States (up from 17 percent in 1990 and 8 percent in 1970). However, women accounted for almost half of all ob-gyns (44 percent) and are soon to be-come the majority, given that 61 percent of all female ob-gyns are located in the youngest third of their workforce. Ob-gyns have the second-largest proportion of women in their physician ranks after pediatricians, among whom women now outnumber men.[11]

While this feminizing of the ob-gyn ranks changes the culture of prac-tice in certain ways, the sharp increase in all women working outside the home in recent decades may have had an unanticipated effect on phy-sicians' professional lives. In 2007, 71 percent of American women with children younger than eighteen worked outside the home (U.S. Bureau of Labor Statistics, 2008). The majority of physicians I interviewed had young children, and both male and female physicians practicing in conservative parts of the country, where their ability to perform abortions might be particularly constrained, often chose their location in order to be near extended family so that they could have help with the children, as both partners usually worked. Given these geographic constraints, some pro-choice physicians I spoke with had only a few employment options, many of which imposed limitations on abortion practice.

Willing male and female physicians cited similar barriers to abortion practice specifically and autonomy in general. Many newly parenting physicians were looking for the best lifestyle possibilities and the fewest nights per week spent on call in order to maximize time with their families. This often meant joining bigger practices so that multiple physicians were available to share the call schedule. Time considerations combined with the fragility of solo and small group practices under managed care have led physicians to become employees of already established group or institutional medical entities. Gone are the days of physicians partnering with like-minded colleagues to form their ideal practice. New physicians leaving residency have learned to expect a different world of medicine.

To Be or Not to Be an Abortion Provider

While physicians in this study who got abortion training may be "your average ob-gyns," the physicians who continued to provide abortion were not. Given the social context of abortion care and the diminished autonomy physicians enjoy, abortion-providing physicians were highly motivated. This finding is corroborated by a national survey of ob-gyns showing that those still performing elective abortions after graduating had a high degree of ideological commitment to the work (Steinauer et al. 2008). Thus, physicians rarely provide abortions without some level of moral, ethical, and/or philosophical motivation. However, the reverse is not true. Willing but unable physicians explain throughout this book that *not* providing abortions says little about one's ideology.

This may seem obvious in other work contexts. For example, the fact that I do not currently teach undergraduate courses does not imply that I have an ideological opposition to undergraduate education. However, physicians I spoke with were trained to do one of the most common procedures within their specialty. They had the hopes and dreams of a social movement conveyed to them through their teachers; that is, residency faculty usually understood that patients' access to abortion was decreasing and urged the graduates to become the next generation of providers. Some were taught quite specifically how to integrate abortion into their clinical practices. Yet my conversations with physicians were marked by expressions of guilt, frustration, and/or explanations about why they had largely discontinued abortion practice, demonstrating that politics and practice are not tied in this context. Physicians I spoke with showed in multiple ways that pro-choice ideology does not necessarily lead to abortion provision.

On Sunday, May 31, 2009, two and a half years after my interviews were completed, Dr. George Tiller, an abortion provider long targeted by antiabortion activists, was shot and killed while ushering at his church in Wichita, Kansas. Dr. Tiller's assassination ended an eleven-year hiatus in physician murders, the last of which took place in 1998, when Dr. Barnett Slepian was shot by a sniper in his kitchen in Buffalo, New York. Such violence clearly deters many physicians from providing abortion; however, the strength of violence as a deterrent to abortion provision was difficult to measure in my study. Those who did residency in the Northeast appeared relatively more fearful of it than the other physicians I spoke with, most likely because they trained during the mid-1990s when a physician was shot in a nearby abortion clinic. The other physicians in the study mentioned violence less than I had expected, and they tended to emphasize barriers presented by the professional culture around abortion practice much more. This finding is especially significant because professional culture, and especially structures that shape professional culture, can be more readily modified than extremist social movements. Sadly, violence against abortion providers seems to be on the rise, and some attribute this to the hopelessness felt by extremists within the antiabortion movement after they lost their antiabortion allies in the White House with the departure of George W. Bush. It is fair to say that some physicians may find the threat of violence to abortion providers more imminent today after the murder of Dr. Tiller than during my interviews. However, regardless of the frightening violence from antiabortion extremists, the reasons many willing physicians cite for not providing abortion relate to subtler barriers that can be addressed from within medicine. In all likelihood, physicians can do more to effect change among their colleagues than they can to effect change among antiabortion extremists.

A Different Moral Dilemma

Dr. Chasey trained at a time when doctors were perceived as godlike, or perhaps as somewhat akin to clergy. They were powerful and did not have as many people looking over their shoulders as they do today. Even when abortion was illegal, physicians faced a very different kind of equation than physicians face today in their decision making about abortion provision. The decision to provide abortion was one that could save lives; the risks were high, but so was the criticalness of the task. Today's physician is less highly revered and less autonomous. Furthermore, abortion is legal, albeit decreasingly accessible in many parts of the country. Therefore, when a doctor is making the calculation about whether to provide an abortion, a woman's life is not necessarily in jeopardy, as it once was. The risks are less stark (less criminal, more professional), but the motive is not as strong. Why risk professional consequences if a woman can get an abortion by driving a few hours away? Why risk professional failure if the motivation is abstract (such as professional obligation) and not concrete (life or death)?

Abortion work clearly presents moral dilemmas, but they are not necessarily those that might be expected. To be sure, some physicians are opposed to performing abortions, but a multitude of individual- and institutional-level protections (frequently called *conscience clauses*) are in place to ensure that health-care providers have the right not to perform or even assist in procedures if they do not want to. Some physicians are troubled by certain aspects of abortion work and yet entirely comfortable with other aspects. Their voices emerge throughout this book in regard to the boundaries that physicians establish around their participation in abortion care and why. However, the moral dilemmas presented by the willing physicians in this book primarily relate to how physicians should react to constraints upon abortion care. Should physicians quit otherwise good jobs where abortion is prohibited? Should they take up battles with senior practice members or hospital administrators over the issue? Should they put their private practices at risk of contention, financial failure, or both by integrating abortion into their work? Are they acting unethically when a woman must travel one, five, or ten hours to get a procedure that they are very well trained to do? Should physicians move to an area of the country where abortion provision is scarce to put their abortion training to good use? How much risk and discomfort should they impose on their family and professional lives for this cause?

After interviewing Dr. Chasey and the physicians who trained with him before he retired, I sometimes wondered what he would have thought about particular circumstances that shaped the choices his trainees had made. As I learned the details of their professional lives after leaving his clinic, and as I analyzed their interpretations of events, I came to see these physicians as individuals who unexpectedly may be facing more complex structural constraints on abortion care than their counterparts of the 1960s and 1970s. Perhaps a few of them lacked "guts." It is hard to say. But rather than individual failings, I saw a group of physicians who shared priorities—children, mortgages, professional success—that could be affected by the decision to provide abortion. And while several of these physicians would have liked to continue to perform abortions after residency and even took steps toward it, they found that there would be significant professional and social costs in doing so—costs that they were not willing to bear. Despite increasing numbers of willing, trained physicians, the barriers erected and continually reinforced within the medical profession are what ultimately restrict women's access to abortion. The constraints faced by the physicians in this book sometimes differed by geographic location, local medical structure, and political climate, but all were born of the stigma and politics of abortion for which American medicine has proved a weak adversary.

CHAPTER 2

Abortion in American Medicine: A Recent History

In 1995, Dr. Jane Hodgson, abortion provider and heroine in the movement to legalize abortion, wrote an editorial in the *British Medical Journal* reflecting on the period of legalized abortion in the United States.[1] In it she lamented the problems that plagued abortion care—problems that, unlike antiabortion activism, were fostered within American medicine itself:

> The public should have been taught by medical leaders for the past 22 years that abortion is a necessary surgical service that should be available to whoever needs it. Abortion clinics should have been encouraged to occupy space in the large professional medical buildings, surrounded by other specialties, or, even better yet, to seek the protection of anonymity within hospital walls. Instead they have been forced into isolation as freestanding clinics. Removed from the mainstream of medical practice, they are more vulnerable to violence and harassment and less accessible to students and residents for the purposes of medical education. (Hodgson 1995: 548)

Dr. Hodgson's words represent the very heart of a prominent pro-choice argument for the integration of abortion services into mainstream health care. Integrationists want to see the medical profession use its muscle to protect and normalize abortion care. Yet, although increases in abortion training since Hodgson wrote her editorial have successfully changed the medical culture of some academic medical settings, little has changed in the overall organization of abortion services. This chapter examines the medical context of abortion practice since *Roe v. Wade*—both how the marginalization of abortion services came about, and solutions advanced by pro-choice advocates and medical constituencies to bring abortion in from the periphery.

Medical leaders have been present and influential in all major stages in U.S. abortion history, including the criminalization of abortion during the nineteenth century, the illegal practice of abortion during the twentieth century, the legalization of abortion in 1973, and the persistent "abortion wars" that have followed. In each of these stages, the medical profession became interested in abortion at times when it assisted the professionalization project—that is, when it could be used to help legitimize its claims to power. Thus, abortion care has not always been "untouchable" by the mainstream. However, given the larger threats to medical autonomy after abortion became legal, abortion services seemed to garner support from mainstream medical associations only at moments when medical autonomy was threatened. Through examination of significant moments of abortion turf grabbing and guarding, one can see that not only is the medical profession's development important to the history of abortion, but abortion is important to the history of the medical profession.

American medicine's relationship to abortion has been one marked by long-standing lethargy (Hodgson 1995), deep ambivalence (Joffe 1995), and even intentional avoidance (Halfmann 2003). Such characterizations should be unsurprising, as American medicine is not a monolithic entity. It is composed of disparate professionals with different political and religious leanings. However, the net effect of the medical profession's noncommittal orientation toward abortion care has been to thwart efforts by abortion rights advocates within medicine to legitimize abortion as a normal reproductive health need. Since abortion was legalized in 1973, the lack of mainstream institutional and organizational support for it (Joffe, Anderson, and Steinauer 1998; Joffe 1995) has ultimately resulted in the marginalization of abortion care into freestanding abortion clinics served by politically motivated physicians. Heated contention around abortion has surfaced within the medical profession periodically over the years, and as this book demonstrates, mainstream medical settings have responded by avoiding involvement with abortion whenever possible. Such avoidance might not be significant if abortion were not one of the most common surgical procedures performed on women of reproductive age (DeFrances and Hall 2007; Jones et al. 2008).

When those in the medical profession have not avoided the discussion of abortion, their positions on it have taken different forms. The most consistent message has been, "no one but us should do it." The medical profession has exerted considerable effort toward ensuring that abortion stay under the domain of physicians—and not the midwives of the nineteenth century or the "back-alley butchers" of the twentieth. The twenty-first-century struggle under way involves midlevel providers working through sanctioned legal and medical channels for the right to provide abortions (not always under the supervision of physicians) in order to expand the base of abortion providers.[2]

Regardless of medicine's interest in maintaining abortion turf, recent decades witnessed a steady decrease in the number of physicians providing abortion in their private practices and hospitals and increased consolidation of abortion services into the socially insulated settings of abortion clinics and academic teaching programs. Although specialized abortion clinics, which provide 93 percent of abortions (Jones et al. 2008), are known to provide efficient and competent care, they are largely segregated from mainstream medicine and reflect the intense marginalization of the stigmatized, uphill battle of abortion practice. The physicians who do the majority of the abortion work in the United States often sacrifice the rest of the skills for which they were trained because multiple forces limit their ability to straddle both the world of mainstream medicine and the world of abortion care.

The Marginalization of Legal Abortion (1973–1985)

In 1973 *Roe v. Wade* legalized abortion nationally, and American medicine was faced with the job of determining how abortion care would be delivered. Had abortion been like any other procedure, without the moral tensions and gender politics that surround it, it would have been one more surgery that physicians would add to their repertoire to be scheduled in hospitals or sometimes done in their offices. If abortion had been legalized during our current era of hyperspecialized medicine, perhaps an outpatient model would have arisen regardless of the politics, but this trend in medicine had not become the norm until at least a decade later. Because abortion is (and has always been) wrapped in such contentious politics, it became an inadvertent trailblazer modeling specialization in outpatient care.

Outpatient abortion services rapidly expanded in the early to mid-1970s. While only thirteen thousand legal abortions were reported to the CDC for the year 1969 (Lindheim 1979), only three years after legalization 1.2 million procedures were reported (Ventura et al. 2000).[3] Regardless of the fact that abortion quickly became and remained extraordinarily common, it was not seamlessly integrated into mainstream medical practice or education. After the *Roe* decision repealed abortion laws, hospitals did not increase their abortion services. Studies from the CDC and Alan Guttmacher Institute (which is now a major authority on national and international reproductive public health research and statistics, founded by the aforementioned physician activist) showed that in the aftermath of *Roe* a minority of doctors and hospitals were involved with abortion care (Jaffe, Lindheim, and Lee 1981: 32). Instead, abortion increasingly took place in clinics modeled after Preterm (one of the first large-scale abortion services, established in Washington, D.C., in 1971) and other legalized abortion services established in states that had already legalized abortion a few years before *Roe*. Typically, such clinics were physically removed from other medical institutions and specialized in abortion with counseling geared toward the social issues surrounding women's experiences with abortion similar to the one Carole Joffe's ethnography documented in the late 1970s (Joffe 1986).

A 1976 study of the responses of major medical associations to the change in abortion law found that twenty-two of the thirty-six responding groups, including the Association of American Medical Colleges, the Joint Commission on Accreditation of Hospitals, and the National Board of Medical Examiners, provided no guidelines regarding the standards of abortion care or recommendations that would normally be expected under such circumstances of major medical policy change (Jaffe, Lindheim, and Lee 1981: 46). Therefore, abortion was not sanctioned as "normal" by these organizations, thus further challenging the legitimacy of abortion services.

The most influential physician organization, the AMA, had treated abortion as a low-priority issue during the legalization process. In this they lagged behind medical organizations, such as the American Public Health Association (APHA) and the American College of Obstetrics and Gynecology (ACOG), in demonstrating support for legalization,[4] even declining to submit an amicus brief directly requested by *Roe v. Wade* attorneys (Halfmann 2003). AMA policymakers told Drew Halfmann (2003), who researched abortion policy trajectories in the United States and Britain, that abortion had not been a high priority around the time of *Roe* because of pressing issues related to soaring health care and malpractice costs and the newly emerging precursors to managed care. Statements made by the AMA on abortion were oriented toward protecting physicians' rights to abstain from performing abortions.[5]

Indeed, the *Roe* decision itself was focused more on ensuring the autonomy of physicians than on ensuring the autonomy of women. The justices who authored the decision intentionally abdicated responsibility to physicians for the larger ethical and moral questions around abortion (Hunter 2006). They did this by insisting that the law protect the privacy of the patient–physician relationship, consistent with earlier contraceptive legislation.[6] The justices held that members of the medical profession possessed health expertise, including the unique ability to decide when an abortion should be performed, and were therefore beyond the purview of legislation. The justices valued medical authority and regarded medicine as a body that should govern itself free from state influence (Hunter 2006). In this way, the legal opinion reflected the professional autonomy that physicians still enjoyed at that time and entrusted physicians, rather than pregnant women, with the moral authority to evaluate the necessity of abortion in each case.

Regardless of abortion's newfound legal status, physicians who had been providing abortions illegally were not readily absorbed into academic departments or residencies to share their skills after *Roe* passed (Joffe 1995). Instead, they remained associated with pre-*Roe* "back-alley butchers" and the controversy surrounding the legalization of abortion and received little support from the preeminent medical organizations. In Carole Joffe's interviews with physicians who provided abortion before and after legalization, providers recounted experiences of being denied surgical privileges at hospitals, skipped over for anticipated medical leadership positions, and excluded from medical societies (Joffe 1995). During these critical early years, academic institutions conducted little training or research in freestanding clinics, and prominent physicians rarely devoted time to working in them (Joffe, Anderson, and Steinauer 1998).

Over the decades since *Roe*, hospital abortion services have steadily decreased. In comparison to the way birth was subsumed and medicalized by the medical profession (Reissman 1998; Sullivan and Weitz 1988), abortion experienced almost the opposite trajectory. Abortion turf seemed to have lost its appeal as it was gradually excised from mainstream medicine, leading to the near-total segregation of abortion care to freestanding clinics. Although in 1976, hospital-based clinics accounted for two-thirds of all abortion providers and one-third of all abortion procedures (Forrest, Tietze, and Sullivan 1978), in 2005 they accounted for just one-third of providers and performed only 5 percent of abortion procedures (Jones et al. 2008). With only 2 percent of abortions taking place in physicians' offices, more than 93 percent of abortion procedures in 2005 took place in specialized abortion clinics dedicated almost exclusively to abortion and contraceptive services (Jones et al. 2008).

In summary, upon the rapid expansion of demand for abortion services after legalization, mainstream medicine largely avoided the job, and specialized abortion clinics arose to meet the need. Major medical associations and regulatory bodies were quiet during abortion policy change and implementation. In avoiding responsibility for abortion care, the American medical profession conveyed to those performing and seeking abortions that it was not sanctioned, normal medical work and that physicians were not professionally obligated to provide abortions.

The Consequences of Isolated Abortion Practice

Marginalization has had detrimental consequences for abortion care. While freestanding abortion clinics were (and still are) generally efficient at delivering quality reproductive health services, their visibility and isolation became a liability during the Reagan-Bush era with the rise of the loud and at times violent antiabortion movement. From 1977 to 2009, forty-one bombings and 175 arson incidents were reported to the police, along with several hundred incidents of burglary, stalking, bomb threats, and anthrax threats. Since 1993, there have been eight murders and seventeen attempted murders of abortion clinic workers and physicians.[7] Clinics have been regularly picketed, with patients and staff members harassed on their way in and out. Protesters successfully popularized imagery of dismembered fetuses on their signs. Ultimately, the antiabortion movement made enormous gains through media portrayals, violence, and obstructive theatrics. Faye Ginsburg, an ethnographer of abortion clinic life, writes about the violence at its peak, "This sense of marginalization and even danger was made stunningly apparent between March 1993 and December 1994 when five people—abortion doctors, clinic staff, and volunteers—were murdered by antiabortion extremists" (Ginsburg 1998: x). In 1994, as a response to this elevation of violence, the Freedom of Access to Clinic Entrances (FACE) Act was passed by the U.S. Congress and signed into law by President Bill Clinton. This provided legal protection to clinics and some degree of deterrence, as the incidence of violence and harassment notably declined.[8]

In the 1990s and 2000s, legislative attacks surpassed violent ones as a means of disrupting or deterring abortion provision. Abortion has been in the courts continuously since it was legalized, as individual lawsuits were brought to whittle away at abortion rights. *Planned Parenthood of Southeastern Pennsylvania v. Casey* in 1992 was particularly significant because it ruled that state authority supersedes the physician authority granted in *Roe.* Hence, it allowed states to create laws affecting patient care. Each year hundreds of bills related to abortion care are filed across the country (Connolly 2005; Donohoe 2005). As of September 2009, thirty-two states have banned the use of state funds for abortion. Specific counseling is mandated in seventeen states, often to inform women of purported consequences of abortion that have been discredited in the scientific literature (breast cancer, mental illness). Twenty-four states require waiting periods, usually twenty-four hours, between the counseling appointment and the procedures. Parental consent and involvement laws exist in thirty-five states.[9]

Furthermore, a trend of what pro-choice organizations call TRAP (Targeted Regulation of Abortion Providers) laws followed in thirty-three states. These are laws designed to make abortion provision prohibitively cumbersome, and they generally apply only to abortion service facilities. While some were purportedly passed to make abortion safer (even though abortion clinics in general have a superb safety record), examples such as laws pertaining to the landscaping of the facility and some architectural requirements seem only to add cost with little benefit to patients (Rose 2007). Some TRAP laws require that registered nurses carry out functions for which, abortion providers claim, nurses are overqualified— even though nurses are in short supply (CRR 2007). Other TRAP laws authorize unannounced inspections of facilities when patients are present, compromising patient confidentiality (CRR 2007).

The isolation of freestanding clinics has been a problem in other ways beyond susceptibility to antiabortion intimidation by protests, violence, and TRAP laws. As early as 1979, abortion researcher Barbara Lindheim articulated her concerns about how confinement to this setting might compromise abortion services and education: "In spite of the generally excellent record of clinics, the estrangement of mainstream health providers from the provision of abortion is of concern. It hinders better integration of health services and makes the development of adequate referral and informational resources of abortion more difficult. By isolating some abortion providers, it decreases opportunities for the professional interaction vital for continuing education and professional self-regulation" (Lindheim 1979: 289). Just as Lindheim suggested, providers have had to advance abortion practice and research in isolation. In order to address problems related to such marginalization, abortion rights activists, including physicians, created the National Abortion Federation (NAF) in 1977. NAF offers practical support and holds conferences every year for abortion providers to share technical knowledge, research findings, and policy concerns. NAF fills the gap left by research institutions and governmental bodies that are normally involved with other medical and public health issues.

Since the 1990s, abortion rights activists and organizations have worked to undo this marginalization and all of its accompanying problems. Groups such as Physicians for Reproductive Choice and Health and Medical Students for Choice especially have called for integration of abortion into the rest of women's health care by mainstream medicine.[10] These integrationists, like Jane Hodgson, argue that physicians could absorb some of the abortion clinic load into their general practices and effectively disperse the targets of violence, increase the number of abortion providers, and destigmatize the practice of abortion.

Integration has not been easy for a host of reasons, some of which are discussed in great detail in this book. A meta-theme affecting all aspects of medical practice, which lacks sufficient recognition by the integration movement, is the restructuring of medicine since the advent of managed care. Studies of physician employment characteristics have consistently demonstrated a trend toward larger group practices as well as significant increases in physicians working as wage and salaried employees without ownership stakes in the group, hospital, or HMO.[11] The trend away from individual and small group ownership has reduced physicians' autonomy over what they do in their practices.

Even when managing bodies have no restrictions on abortion, the low cost of abortion is a further deterrent to integration. The cost of abortion has been suppressed since the 1970s because of the high efficiency of specialized clinics (some for-profit ones are derogatorily called "abortion mills"). Additionally, a combination of pro-choice philanthropy and volunteerism has subsidized abortion costs in nonprofit clinics in order to make abortion more accessible and affordable for patients. Thus insurance reimbursements are low, and physicians (or their business managers) feel they "lose" money by performing abortions when compared with what they would earn doing other procedures that take the same amount of time and resources. Thus, abortion clinics fit perfectly with the ever-increasing trend under managed care to contract out specialized work, saving managing bodies money. Therefore, under managed care, physicians (outside of abortion clinics and academia) often lack control over whether to include abortion in their practices for financial reasons in addition to ideological ones.

Abortion rights advocates, however, hopeful that motivated physicians can overcome these constraints, have focused on how to increase the supply of *willing* providers. In particular, medical student and resident training became a strategic focus of institutional (as opposed to grassroots) abortion rights activism during the 1990s, as it seemed the most clearly modifiable factor within medicine. Abortion training was not strong in residency curriculums after legalization, and it had become increasingly sparse as antiabortion controversy and violence escalated. Between 1985 and 1991, the proportion of ob-gyn residency programs that routinely offered training in first-trimester abortions decreased from 23 percent (Darney et al. 1987) to 12 percent (MacKay and MacKay 1995). Given that abortion was more common than hysterectomy, sterilization, or C-section (ACS 1993; Owings and Kozak 1998) during this period, the dearth of training in abortion care in ob-gyn residency programs became a concern to a wider audience beyond abortion rights advocates, most notably the Accreditation Council of Graduate Medical Education (ACGME).

Of additional concern, many physicians who had dedicated their careers to abortion since *Roe* were retiring, and in the increasingly hostile political climate, few were filling their shoes. In 1990, NAF organized a symposium to explore "key reasons underlying the lack of available abortion providers and to develop strategies to address this situation" (Joffe, Anderson, and Steinauer 1998: 323). For the first time ever, representatives were sent to a NAF event from ACOG (which cosponsored the symposium), the ACGME, and the Council on Resident Education in Obstetrics and Gynecology. The symposium concluded that several factors were contributing to the abortion provider shortage: "Among those noted were the 'graying' of abortion providers who had come of age in the pre-*Roe* era and had seen the ravages of illegal abortion, increasing anti-abortion harassment and violence, inadequate economic incentives for abortion work, and the social stigma and professional isolation that commonly accompanied abortion work" (Joffe, Anderson, and Steinauer 1998: 323). The professional isolation noted here refers to the fact that abortion providers frequently give up mainstream medicine (often not voluntarily) to work in abortion clinics. This means they sacrifice the majority of what they were trained for, such as preventive care, birth, and gynecological surgeries. Full-spectrum care necessitates working in a hospital setting and interacting with diverse personnel in addition to attending professional meetings with colleagues. Abortion clinic physicians, on the other hand, tend to have relatively less contact with other physicians.

Thus, at the same time that managed care redistributed power in U.S. medicine, abortion care suffered multiple blows. With abortion contention at its highest, antiabortion harassment, legislative attacks, increased professional isolation, and decreased abortion training in residency resulted in a declining provider base. The isolated, marginalized abortion services continued as such as they fit neatly into the newly dominating structure of medical subspecialization and outsourced care.

Mobilizing around Abortion: A Fight for Professional Authority

While the marginalization of abortion services has continued largely uncontested by the medical profession, three head-on conflicts over abortion regulation united major medical powers in recent years when medical authority has felt most threatened. These encounters to some extent represented a partisan political battle of pro-choice doctors against anti-abortion political constituents. But the ability of vocal pro-choice physicians to enlist wider support represents an unprecedented willingness of the professional associations to get involved and put their names behind abortion as an issue.

The first battle took place over training requirements. In 1995, after five years of research and consultation with residencies and other medical organizations, the ACGME approved new standards for residency education that would require training in abortion and the management of abortion-related complications, barring moral or religious objections from the individual resident or hospital. This unleashed a strong response from members of the U.S. Congress, who made every attempt to impede the new ACGME requirements. In a rare moment of medical mobilization, representatives from the AMA, ACOG, and a handful of other medical organizations defended the new standards (Joffe, Anderson, and Steinauer 1998). They were particularly vocal against governmental intrusion into the medical profession's private regulatory bodies. On June 14, 1995, a representative of ACOG, Dr. Frank Ling, argued before the House of Representatives: "Congressional override of the ACGME requirements would represent an unprecedented involvement in the private educational accreditation process. Never before has such an override of education standards been proposed . . . Congress is simply not equipped to make decisions about what is or is not appropriate medical care and training" (cited in Joffe, Anderson, and Steinauer 1998: 326).

Accustomed to self-regulation in this regard, the major medical groups saw this as a flagrant intrusion of politics into their domain. The timing of this battle is interesting in that it occurred at the height of discontent with and moral outrage about managed care. Thus, while the medical profession had lost much control around how medicine is practiced, it held tightly onto its relatively intact ability to regulate its educational and training requirements. The ACGME mandate took effect January 1, 1996, but Congress made that mandate difficult to enforce by passing the Coats Amendment to the Omnibus Consolidated Rescissions and Appropriations Act of 1996 (Public Law 104-134), which ensures that "residency programs will be deemed accredited by the federal government, or any state or local government that receives federal funds, even if programs fail to comply with abortion training accreditation requirements" (Foster, van Dis, and Steinauer 2003: 1777). Additionally, several states passed legislation prohibiting elective abortion in publicly supported institutions, which made it necessary for their residency programs to train residents at off-site abortion clinics to stay in compliance with the ACGME requirements (Foster, van Dis, and Steinauer 2003). Ironically, the fight with Congress over the ACGME mandate presented a professionalization opportunity similar to the one provided by the nineteenth-century criminalization of abortion. While a century earlier physicians rallied behind the campaign to criminalize abortion to build professional authority, here, too, in 1995 physicians rallied around abortion to strengthen their power, although they were on the opposite side of the issue.

The second case of medical mobilization around abortion took place a decade later. Major medical associations came together to oppose a Supreme Court ban on "partial-birth" abortion, a specific technique of second-trimester abortion that its opponents construed as inhumane (it is sometimes called D&X, for dilation and extraction, in the medical community).[12] In this case, medical professionals strongly objected to governmental regulation of the surgical technique. Specifically, what was at stake was the fact that the law had no health or life exemption for the pregnant woman, meaning that the procedure would be banned even if a physician believed it to be the safest way to terminate a pregnancy for a particular case. ACOG offered a statement that in some cases D&X "may be the best or most appropriate procedure . . . to save the life or preserve the health of a woman," and several experienced abortion providers testified thus (*Gonzales v. Carhart* 2007). However, antiabortion physicians selected by the Bush administration argued both that it was inhumane and that it was never necessary. Interestingly, these physicians had never performed such abortions because of their political positions on the issue, but the testimonies of physicians who were experts in abortion care were deemed too biased to be credible, making for a particularly problematic construction of expertise characteristic of the Bush era.[13] Bioethics lawyer Alta Charo concluded in an editorial: "The Court then argued that since medical opinion is divided about D&X, Congress has the authority to invade the doctor–patient relationship and substitute blanket judgment for individualized medical judgment concerning the best care for a particular patient. Although regulation of the drugs and devices marketed for use in medical care has long been accepted, legislative restriction of doctors' individual medical judgment is far more contentious" (Charo 2007: 2127). It is noteworthy that this nearly scathing response was found in arguably the most prestigious medical journal in the United States, the *New England Journal of Medicine*. It was presented in a special edition with other like-minded editorials, including one entitled "The Intimidation of American Physicians: Banning Partial-Birth Abortion" (Greene 2007). Dr. Michael Greene writes: "The decision to pursue a second-trimester abortion is never taken lightly and usually results only after anguished discussions among the patient, her loved ones, and her health care providers . . . the last thing a provider needs is to have to worry that the procedure could potentially evolve into a criminal act if a fetus in breech presentation should slip out intact through a partially dilated cervix. But this is exactly the situation created by the partial-birth abortion bill" (Greene 2007: 2128). Greene was not alone; other physicians shared his fears of accidentally breaking the law and facing prosecution. One physician I interviewed panicked when scheduling a second-trimester abortion procedure at her hospital, scared that she might be prosecuted as she second-guessed the distinction between a "normal" second-trimester abortion and a "partial-birth" abortion (see a more detailed account in Chapter 5), while another worried that "they could manipulate the wording to get rid of first-trimesters too." Thus, the ban resulted in the insecurity of physicians vis-à-vis the government in a way that is reminiscent of earlier years of illegal abortion practice.

The third and most recent incident was sparked by an ACOG (2007) report entitled "The Limits of Conscience Refusal in Reproductive Medicine." It relates to "refusal" or "conscience" clauses in legislation that have popped up throughout the United States. These clauses protect both individuals and institutions from legal liability when they abstain from abortion provision or a variety of things they find objectionable (contraception, sterilization, emergency contraception, etc.). The "right to refuse" has been extended in practice to giving referrals and information as well (Curlin et al. 2007). The ACOG report stated, "Physicians and other health care professionals have the duty to refer patients in a timely manner to other providers if they do not feel that they can in conscience provide the standard reproductive service that patients request" (ACOG 2007: 5). In doing this, ACOG took a firm stance on a politically inflammatory matter. Its claims assert that physicians have a professional obligation to their patients related to contested aspects of reproductive health care.

The report generated a response from Health and Human Services Secretary Mike Leavitt—former governor of Utah appointed by George W. Bush in 2005—in the form of a press release in which he made explicit his disappointment in ACOG's new policy, going so far as to call on the American Board of Obstetrics and Gynecology (ABOG) responsible for physician certification and licensing to reject the policy and "protect the conscience rights of physicians."[14] In a letter Leavitt wrote to ABOG that was included with the press release, he stated, "I am concerned that the actions taken by ACOG and ABOG could result in the denial or revocation of Board certification of a physician who—but for his or her refusal, for example, to refer a patient for an abortion—would be certified." Thus, in December 2008, in the final weeks of Bush's presidency, he signed into law an additional "conscience" protection for health-care practitioners who violate ACOG's referral requirement policy. Seven states filed lawsuits against Health and Human Services as a response, and soon after President Barack Obama took office, his administration began working to revoke the Bush rule, citing concerns over health-care access (Sorrell 2009).

These three incidences mark significant points of recent contact between governing and medical authorities over abortion. While the politics of abortion are the driving force behind these debates, it is notable that the medical profession has had relatively little interest in direct involvement with abortion care until the government threatened medical autonomy. In these cases, physicians did not overtly embrace the politics of reproductive rights, but they did argue on behalf of the quality of abortion care. These battles represented something vital to the profession, their last vestige: control over the content (if not the business) of medicine.

Today: Abortion Training and the Provider Shortage

Finding physicians who are willing to provide abortions in the current political and medical context can be challenging in some parts of the country, especially rural areas. Abortion rights advocates within medicine have focused on improving abortion training in residency programs because increasing the supply of physicians means improving access to abortion for patients. Since the ACGME mandated abortion training in residency in 1996, a study showed that 46 percent of residencies—up from 12 percent before the mandate (MacKay and MacKay 1995)—claim to offer "routine training" in abortion (Almeling, Tews, and Dudley 2000), but the same study showed such low rates of residents getting trained that it brought that study's definition of "routine training" into question (Landy and Steinauer 2001).

Routine training and *opt-out training* are terms used to indicate that abortion training is included within the normal curriculum of a residency program and that if a resident does not want to be trained in abortion care, he or she must actively choose not to participate. Although residency programs must comply with the ACGME mandate, most new programs appeared to be offering "opt-in" training, meaning that the resident would need to use his or her elective period to go to a local Planned Parenthood or other off-site outpatient clinic for training. Such abortion clinics can provide thorough training because of the high patient volume; however, when routine training in abortion is integrated into other hospital services, abortion may be viewed less politically and more as a normal part of a spectrum of ob-gyn services. This reasoning implies that the normative function of medical authority extends from residency to resident, not just from physician to patient. Indeed, a study of the effect of training on provision in one state found that "the more integrated and extensive the training, the more likely the graduate is to provide abortions" (Steinauer et al. 2003: 1163). This suggests two things: first, more abortion training makes residents more confident in their abortion skills, and second, more training normalizes the highly stigmatized and contested procedure. The former is expected, but seeing as abortion is a somewhat simple surgery compared with the many learned during residency, normalizing abortion seems to be the more significant accomplishment of increased training.

Recent years have witnessed a steady increase in both programs with routine (now up to 51 percent) and opt-out (39 percent) training (Eastwood et al. 2006) as well as increased resident participation in the abortion training (Steinauer et al. 2007). A national survey of ob-gyns regarding their experiences in abortion training during the 1990s showed that graduates trained after the ACGME requirements went into effect were more likely to perform abortions (Steinauer et al. 2007). This finding indicates that the official policy change (and the programmatic changes that resulted from it) increased their acceptance of abortion practice.

Regardless of improvements in training, the overall number of providers continues to decrease nationally, though the decline has slowed its pace. The number of providers declined by 14 percent from 1992 to 1996, 11 percent from 1996 to 2000, and only 2 percent from 2000 to 2005 (Jones et al. 2008). In 2005, 69 percent of metropolitan counties in the United States and 97 percent of nonmetropolitan counties had no abortion provider at all (Jones et al. 2008). Medication abortion—also known as the French abortion pill or RU-486,[15] approved in 2000 for use in the United States—has slowly changed some of the culture of abortion care such that it now accounts for 13 percent of procedures (Jones et al. 2008), but the vast majority of these are performed in abortion clinics and not integrated into primary care or rural health care at the rates that pro-choice advocates initially hoped (Joffe and Weitz 2003; Shochet and Trussell 2008). Physicians are not in short supply for most urban abortion clinics, but rural clinics and those in conservative semi-urban areas struggle to find physicians and often rely on physicians who are willing to commute by airplane part time.[16] Therefore, the provider shortage is predominant in rural and conservative towns.

Summary

After *Roe v. Wade* legalized abortion in 1973, services expanded rapidly, but largely at the margins of medicine. Mainstream medicine had little response and grew decreasingly involved with abortion care, sending the message that abortion was not a normal part of women's health care, that it was political and separate. In its marginalization, abortion care was vulnerable to the ideological contention surrounding it, which brought harassment, legislative barriers to care, professional isolation, and little support for training new providers. At the same time, managed care was revolutionizing the structure of medicine and in the process decreasing physician autonomy such that physicians were less able to provide abortions within their general practices even if they wanted to. Finally, as a specialized service, the abortion clinic model fit neatly into the managed care model, which was increasingly contracting out specific services to save money.

By and large, major medical professional organizations were passive about how marginalization was affecting abortion services. However, they became active around abortion at key moments when conservative political attempts to suppress abortion affected the profession's ability to regulate the technical and educational content of medicine. In order to protect their ability to control the parameters of abortion training (ACGME mandate), surgical technique (partial-birth abortion), and professional obligation (limiting conscience clauses), medical associations were willing to involve themselves with abortion once again.

CHAPTER 3

Unwilling, Willing, and Why

A recent national survey showed that only 22 percent of ob-gyns in the United States had performed an abortion in the previous year (Steinauer et al. 2008).[1] The same survey also found that, of all ob-gyns who had intended (preresidency) to provide abortions after completion of their training, only half (52 percent) did so. Of those who had *not* intended to perform abortions before residency, 5 percent did anyway. Furthermore, of the group who were undecided before residency, 19 percent went on to provide abortions. These findings suggest that despite conventional wisdom that physicians decide whether or not to provide abortion based on their moral convictions (that is, whether they consider abortion to be "right" or "wrong"), the decision to perform abortions is not so straightforward. Other factors significantly influence whether or not physicians will ultimately provide abortion care after their medical training, including constraints on abortion practice where they work and the extent to which they view abortion care as a professional responsibility.

As already stated, the research for this book was inspired by the need to address the question of what happens after training—out in the "real world" of medical practice—that leads such a small portion of *willing* physicians to perform abortions. I address specific barriers to abortion provision later in the book; here, I describe how the physicians I interviewed think about their professional obligation to provide abortions and what bearing that has (if any) on their willingness to do so. Because of the unusual social conditions around abortion, practice preferences vary widely. Some physicians wish they could perform abortions but are limited by prohibitions on abortion where they work, while some physicians prefer as little contact with abortion as possible, and still others perform abortions as the majority of their practice. For discussion here, I divide the group into *unwilling* and *willing* physicians. In the unwilling group, I include those who declined abortion training and those who were trained but concluded after residency that they were morally uncomfortable with or opposed to abortion for various reasons. The willing physicians, on the other hand, are those who were both supportive of abortion rights and amenable to including abortion care in their practices; however, some were *able* and some were *unable* to provide abortions. In many cases, able and unable physicians looked ideologically and philosophically identical, differentiated only by the constraints of their practice environments. In other cases, the degree to which these physicians embraced abortion provision as their professional obligation to patients was quite different.

The social construction of the term *abortion provider* adds complexity to these distinctions. Some unwilling doctors and many of the willing-unable ones in fact occasionally performed or assisted in abortion procedures in very specific (often more socially acceptable) cases, usually when the patient was well known to them and had received a diagnosis of a serious fetal anomaly. However, because these cases were relatively rare and because these physicians did not identify themselves as abortion providers (because they were either unwilling or unable to perform abortions for most patients), I do not refer to them as abortion providers.

I categorize physician respondents on the basis of willingness here in order to help separate, for analytical purposes, the varying extents to which they feel it is their medical duty or obligation to society to address the public health, moral, and social justice imperatives of abortion through their work. These various imperatives underlie the larger social problem of abortion—one of the most persistently controversial issues in American politics and society. Americans fight endlessly about how to answer the following questions: Is abortion a valid solution to an unwanted (or unhealthy) pregnancy? Is it moral? Is it a woman's right? Should society sanction it with legality and funding? Should the medical community support it with training and provision? If abortion is made illegal in the United States, how should society respond to illegal (and unsafe) abortion, which exists in nearly every country where abortion is prohibited? And finally, the question that shapes this research and sets the background to the interviews I conducted with ob-gyns around the country: if abortion is legal but unavailable in the United States, what should physicians do, if anything, to address this? Given that ob-gyns are the specialists of the uterus, the doctors under whose purview abortion falls most concretely,[2] they cannot entirely evade these questions. A close examination of the different perspectives on professional obligation illustrates differences in physician orientation to the controversial subject of abortion beyond the typical moral binaries of pro-life and pro-choice.

Unwilling

Unwilling physicians are those who know at the outset of residency that they want to forgo abortion training (opt-outs) and those who decide after training that they no longer want to perform abortions for moral reasons (although some made exceptions for certain medically or genetically indicated terminations). The four residency programs I studied include abortion training in the curriculum, and therefore, if a physician has a moral objection to such training, he or she must opt out of it. In such cases, residents learn the very same surgical procedure for miscarriages only and do not do elective terminations. This means they are trained in the same methods of cleaning out the uterus but do so much less often, because miscarriages that necessitate surgery are not as frequent or as concentrated for learning purposes as abortions are in an abortion clinic. For example, a patient who miscarries typically shows up in the emergency room and may or may not need a surgical procedure to complete the miscarriage, depending on her medical circumstances. In contrast, an abortion clinic will schedule all the patients for blocks of time such that the resident will do five to fifteen procedures in one day. If residents opt out of abortion training, they will have had training in some of the same skills but may feel less confident because of the lower frequency with which they have used them. There are no other common procedures across subspecialties in medicine that residents regularly opt out of for moral reasons. Abortion is unique in this way.

At first glance, opt-outs might seem to be a homogeneous group; however, the opt-outs I spoke with were morally uncomfortable with or opposed to abortion for different reasons, and their level of opposition also varied. None of the opt-outs I interviewed felt abortion should be illegal. Given that my study primarily addressed abortion training, ob-gyns who were completely opposed to the legality of abortion probably chose not to take part in the study by not returning the consent forms mailed to them. It is for this reason, I believe, that my opt-outs were relatively moderate in their moral discomfort with abortion.

Some opt-outs cited their religious backgrounds as the main reason for not doing abortion procedures. For example, Dr. Francine Gray, an ob-gyn practicing in the South, said that it was "more upbringing" that informed her decision: "I was raised Roman Catholic. So, I'm a practicing Catholic." Dr. Gray did not struggle with the decision to opt out of training; she described it as a matter of course.

For Dr. Vivian Costa, an ob-gyn subspecialist of pelvic floor dysfunction practicing in the Northeast, the decision was not a given and she wrestled with it. Dr. Costa thinks of herself as spiritual but is not affiliated with an organized religion; she ultimately decided against abortion training because she felt "it is an end of life, and while I feel that patients should have an option, I didn't feel comfortable being a provider." For some opt-outs their decision not to participate in abortion training was closely related to their core identity. They thought of themselves as individuals who would not end fetal life. They were not able or willing to bracket that moral discomfort with elective abortion, even temporarily for the purposes of acquiring skills as some others did. However, most of them approved of abortion when the fetus had a severe anomaly (genetic indication) or when the woman's health was at risk from the pregnancy (maternal indication), and some even occasionally performed or assisted in such procedures.

Some physicians opted out of abortion training because they felt it would not benefit them professionally, but this can have moral overtones. For example, Dr. Will Corrigan, a reproductive endocrinologist and infertility specialist practicing in a western city, decided to opt out of abortion training because he felt it did not pertain to him, given his specialty choice. "I knew that I wanted to go into infertility," he said, "and so doing abortions as a part of my practice probably was neither going to be necessary nor probably good for business." On the surface, his decision seemed simply pragmatic. As a physician in the business of helping women get pregnant, why did he need to learn how to terminate pregnancies? However, learning to do dilation and curettage (D&C) is indeed "necessary" for him, as he went on to report: "I do many D&C procedures for miscarriages. I do those all the time." Therefore, technically speaking, training in D&C would be beneficial to an endocrinologist's surgical skills.

With further discussion it became clear that Dr. Corrigan's decision to not participate in abortion training had a more political or moral component than he initially revealed. Indeed, as an infertility specialist he is no stranger to moral dilemmas about embryonic and fetal life.[3] Frequently, patients undergoing in-vitro fertilization end up with more successfully implanted embryos than they wish to carry to term, and some opt to "selectively reduce" the number of embryos in the uterus through fatal injections into some of the embryonic sacs. Dr. Corrigan asserts, however, that he is not morally conflicted by this issue:

> We're involved with the selective reduction, which could be considered a form of abortion. And there are some fertility specialists who are probably, I would say, against [the] selective reduction process . . . I would say for some individuals, not me, it's a source of significant stress to try to balance pregnancy versus terminating some of the pregnancies versus proceeding with the triplet or quadruplet pregnancy. I know that it's a source of stress for one of my other partners, balancing the science with his particular moral beliefs. Not for me.

While he asserts that he is not conflicted by the destruction of embryonic life, the moral conflict for Dr. Corrigan is the behavior of pregnant women. He is regularly exposed to patients who must struggle to become pregnant, and he empathizes with their plight. And in turn, his sympathies wane for those who find themselves with unwanted pregnancies. He talked of the frustrations of his infertility patients when they must come into contact with women seeking abortions—the unfairness and hurtfulness of being around them: "Some patients have said that when they had to, for example, sit in the operating room, or in the waiting room [of the general ob-gyn clinic] knowing that there was a woman sitting next to them . . . saying that she gets pregnant all the time and has had X number of abortions . . . Our patients who [are] experiencing infertility and trying for months or years to try to get pregnant, they—I've seen patients very upset under those circumstances." Dr. Corrigan seems ideologically predisposed to distancing himself from the world of abortion, especially abortions due to accidental pregnancy. His involvement with selective reduction shows that he does not have strong discomfort with pregnancy termination in principle, as did Dr. Gray and Dr. Costa, but he shared their desire to have no direct involvement with elective abortion even during training and exhibited little (if any) sense of professional obligation toward abortion care.

Physicians who became morally conflicted about abortion during or after training are also a diverse group. Such physicians found either the behavior of abortion patients or the abortion itself morally objectionable. Through their experiences as residents serving abortion patients they came to feel burdened, resentful, or overwhelmed, and they ultimately distanced themselves from a professional obligation toward abortion care. These physicians often went through abortion training because they wanted to gain technical expertise in intrauterine surgery, but some lost empathy for abortion patients in the process or became troubled by fetal death more than they had expected and therefore chose to discontinue abortion provision after residency on moral grounds. Many of these physicians held a pro-choice philosophy about abortion—that it should be legal and a personal choice. For some, however, serving patients with whom they did not empathize exacerbated moral ambivalence they had around abortion. For others, the loss of embryonic or fetal life was less tolerable to them than they had initially thought. Dr. Mary White, an ob-gyn now working in a Catholic hospital in the Midwest where abortions are prohibited, hinted at all of these moral discomforts. "I definitely did not like doing the procedure, the abortion," she said. "At the time it was important to learn it . . . you know, it wouldn't be something I'd do myself, have an abortion . . . I feel comfortable with not doing them anymore . . . I had a hard time dealing with women that did use that as their primary form of birth control."

Dr. White's sentiment, that women who had more than one abortion were using it as a "form of birth control," reflects a relatively common critique of the practice of abortion. Those who identify with this critique, in a sense, disparage women for "killing" more than once. One accident is acceptable, but several betray a bad or immoral sensibility. In contrast, physicians who feel empathetic to women commonly referred to in the abortion world as "repeat patients" or "repeaters" are more likely to attribute such women's needs for more abortions to low resources, low education, or lack of empowerment. It can become harder for physicians to accept (if not participate in) fetal death if they resent the patient's behavior, that is, the sexual and reproductive choices the patient made leading up to the abortion.

Morally conflicted physicians were more negative about abortion work and abortion patients after graduating than they were going into residency. The experience of caring for women they judged as irresponsible or perhaps undeserving of help in a sense alienated them from their emotional labor and eroded their sense of professional obligation toward abortion care (Hochschild 1985). Dr. Aaron Sacks thinks of himself as pro-choice, and he felt obligated to share the responsibilities of running the residency program's abortion clinic with his co-residents, but like Dr. White, he disliked doing abortions: "I did, unfortunately, plenty of abortions at [our] hospital in the framework of the residency training . . . We had an option to decline [abortion training], and some of us chose to decline. But I didn't feel like [that would] help any because those will be done in any case. And the other guys who do not decline will have to do more of that. In addition, I was chief administrator to the president and, you know, that wasn't a good personal example." Dr. Sacks makes clear that he finds abortion distasteful by use of the word *unfortunately* and by expressing the desire he held to opt out of training even if he did not do so. His statement also alludes to specific residency politics in that, in some programs, when residents opt out of abortion training, other residents must pick up the slack. He concluded that as a leader in the program, he did not want to exacerbate that problem because of his discomfort with abortion, and "in any case," the same number of abortions would occur regardless of whether he was the one doing them. Essentially, his perspective is that it's a moral wash if the same number of abortions happen, regardless of who does them. Dr. Sacks felt professionally obligated to do his part in the residency program, but he did not have a strong sense of professional obligation toward abortion patients. He went on to say:

> Since finishing residency, I have never done any abortions. I think it has to do with—as much as I would like to say that it's only my practice—but if I really look honestly, I would prefer not to do the abortions because somehow it's difficult for me to draw the line between a child and a fetus and a baby. And all that is semantics to me . . . it touches me somewhere inside. [During training] I tried not to think [about] what I am doing. I just did it in the best technical manner I could do . . . And I was just looking at the end of the day to finish and that's it.

Dr. Sacks explained that he actively tries to appear nonjudgmental about abortion when counseling patients with unwanted pregnancy in his current practice; however, he provides no information about abortion providers or referrals. "I just tell them to look at the yellow book [the yellow pages of the phone book]," he said. "And, you know, if you open the yellow book, on the first or second page, immediately there's this huge ad about abortion."

In a sense, some morally conflicted physicians shared a low-level resentment that they were placed in a position in their servitude as residents to assume the moral burden of solving a woman's problem; in other words, physicians must end fetal life in order to bail a woman out of a situation that might not have existed had she been a "better" person. Therefore, the moral discomfort manifested in two different, but interrelated ways. Some were bothered by fetal death, whereas others were bothered more by women's sexual and maternal behavior. The latter issue, discussed in detail in the introduction, has to do with the way that political debate around abortion is often grounded in gender politics (Luker 1984). Much of what is offensive to people about abortion is the way in which a woman can enjoy the "benefits" of sex without its "consequences," that is, motherhood. This is a belief or morality that many people, sometimes even unlikely candidates such as career-focused female physicians, hold at their core. These two issues, fetal death and women's behavior, become intertwined in this context: if a physician is significantly bothered by fetal death, it is easier to justify doing the procedure when he or she sympathizes with the plight of the patient. And also the converse is true: if such a physician (or most Americans for that matter) cannot relate to the patient, the circumstances of her unwanted pregnancy must not be the result of her sexual choices in order to engender sympathy as with severe genetic anomalies, rape, and incest. Physicians with these moral conflicts regarding patients' sexual behavior seemed to feel less implicated by and less professional responsibility for the problem of the shrinking abortion provider base in the United States. In fact, some seemed to feel themselves "victimized" as physicians by having to perform abortion procedures during training. The result is that these physicians actively distanced themselves from that obligation afterward.

A number of physicians I spoke with were morally conflicted about fetal death more than they were about patient behavior. Generally, they were people who support abortion rights and feel they ideally should continue to provide abortions, but they are very ambivalent about the morality of abortion. They feel professionally implicated by the scarcity of abortion provision that exists in certain regions. Yet, while they want to "put their money where their mouth is," they were at times morally uncomfortable doing the procedure during residency. In a sense, they are politically similar to many willing doctors, but in practice, their moral compass sends them a different message. Some of the morally conflicted doctors went on to provide elective abortions to the occasional patient in their practices with whom they empathized. But generally, those who felt this moral discomfort with fetal death during abortion training decided not to continue to perform elective abortions after residency.

Dr. Tom Burns, an ob-gyn practicing in a southern military facility, for example, describes himself as a social liberal with a conservative foundation. He did a lot of what he described as "soul searching" early in his medical training about whether to do abortions. Inspired by John Irving's popular novel *The Cider House Rules* (1985), whose heroic protagonist performs illegal abortions for women before the *Roe* decision, he went on to participate in abortion training during residency; but when he later went to work for the military, he was allowed to do terminations only for medical and genetic indications:

> I felt very well trained [in abortion care], and I can take good care of the women who desire that option. In a way I kind of felt bad about giving it up because there are not very many people who are well trained in it . . . Unfortunately, my personal beliefs didn't jibe with it. You know, I just didn't feel like I was doing the right thing for myself. It's weird, I'm, like

I said, conservative mainly, but when it comes to kind of social issues like that, I'm liberal . . . [I] believe in a woman's right to choose.

Dr. Burns seemed to go back and forth trying to explain his position on abortion; he was actively conflicted. However, his philosophy might be more internally consistent than he realized. He was committed to personal freedom and autonomy from government regulation (a central tenet of conservative ideology); hence, he supported a woman's right to choose abortion. But he also comes from a conservative religious background and holds the same feelings about fetal life as his parents did: he finds the destruction of it distasteful, or immoral. Working for the military relieved him of the decision to offer elective abortions or not because of the military's stance on abortion.

Dr. Rebecca Holmes, practicing in a suburb of a large northeastern city, had participated in abortion training. She remembered it as both grueling work and exceptional training for her surgical skill development. But she was clear when she finished her training that she would not continue to provide abortions. "I knew I wouldn't," she said. "I just didn't want to. I just did not enjoy pulling the fetus out." Dr. Holmes trained in an inner-city hospital with a busy abortion service that depended entirely on the residents. This resulted in an abortion training experience that was longer and more stressful than average, while serving impoverished patients. Her decision to cease involvement with abortion care was not for lack of empathy for abortion patients. Rather, the intensity of the abortion service in her residency program left little room for emotional detachment (Hochschild 1985; Maslach 1982; Parsons 1951). Dr. Holmes was politically supportive of abortion rights, yet as a physician she felt overwhelmed by the difficulty in patients' lives that related to their abortion decisions. "When someone did decide to go through with the abortion," she said, "I always respected that. Like you're saying, 'Stop now and don't cause this child any pain' . . . That part actually wasn't the problem for me, it wasn't the choice. It was more just the sadness that the mother would, you know, that the child couldn't have a chance . . . And personally, I just didn't want—I just felt like I'd done enough. I just did not want to do them anymore." Ultimately, Dr. Holmes was saying that she could see abortion as a humane choice in many cases, yet she, as the physician, was so saddened by women's circumstances and the loss of life she was seeing, she could not emotionally bear it. Some of this is endemic to the experience of working in the inner city, as she was. Seeing the poorest patients can be both heartbreaking and emotionally draining for physicians of any specialty, largely because so many of the medical problems result from or are made worse by poverty and presumably preventable conditions or behaviors. Dr. Holmes went on to take a job in a suburban private practice that serves an insured, middle- to upper-class population, where she found herself decidedly less overwhelmed.

Unwilling physicians in this study did not want to provide abortion for different but intimately related reasons. Dr. White and Dr. Sacks are pro-choice physicians who initially saw abortion as a professional duty, but they came to resent and judge the patients for what they considered immoral behavior and for "burdening" them with solving their problems, and so they ultimately distanced themselves from a professional obligation to provide abortion. Dr. Burns felt a professional obligation toward providing abortion but struggled unsuccessfully to suppress his moral discomfort with ending fetal life despite his appreciation for the personal freedom to choose abortion. And finally, Dr. Holmes felt she had already fulfilled her professional obligation, having "done her time" in the abortion clinic during residency, and stopped doing abortion—not for lack of empathy, but rather because she felt overwhelmed by it.

Willing-Unable

The majority of physicians I spoke with who would be willing to do abortions in their practices did not do so after residency. Because of the context of abortion care in the United States, willing ob-gyns rarely performed elective abortions after residency, and only occasionally performed genetically and medically indicated ones. Yet, by focusing on physicians' sense of professional duty or obligation rather than their actual provision of abortion care, we can see that these willing yet unable physicians differ from unwilling physicians in meaningful ways. Willing-unable physicians share in common the fact that they are not significantly conflicted about the morality of abortion, and under different conditions, they would gladly perform abortions. In terms of professional obligation, however, they sometimes vary in the degree of responsibility they feel toward it.

Several willing-unable doctors I spoke with regarded their experience with abortion training positively but did not lament discontinuing abortion practice after training. While familiar with the politics surrounding abortion and how abortion providers are diminishing in number, physicians with a relatively low degree of professional obligation toward abortion did not struggle with the question of how to continue to provide abortion after residency and appeared to disassociate themselves from the issue. In fact, a good way to characterize these individuals is by their resistance to feeling implicated by the social problem to which they are decidedly central. They did not feel like powerful agents in the "abortion wars," and therefore, instead of (1) acting to gain more power or (2) emotionally reacting with guilt or regret to their decision not to fight, they separated themselves from the problem.

Some doctors disassociated themselves from the abortion training imperative to continue provision thereafter through an assertion that it was too unsafe, controversial, or stigmatized in their community (as opposed to citing personal moral discomfort). These were concerns that other doctors had as well, but those who disassociated themselves from abortion care seemed to employ them to absolve themselves of responsibility. For example, Dr. Marjorie Peterson, an ob-gyn who practices in a small town in the Midwest and no longer provides abortions, described herself as pro-choice and appreciative of the skills she acquired during abortion training that help her in other aspects of her practice. She was cordial during our telephone interview but very brief in her responses when I asked about her reasons for not doing abortions. She said, for example, that it was "too political" and that it had not been a priority for her to ask about abortion during her job interview process. The only mention of abortion she recalled upon starting her job was on the application to practice in local hospitals. The application listed all of the ob-gyn surgical procedures with empty boxes next to each one for physicians to check if they wanted to be granted permission to perform them. Dr. Peterson remarked matter-of-factly, "Since they're all Catholic hospitals, obviously I would never check that box." This is not something she identified as a problem during our discussion. While other doctors expounded their frustrations about prohibitions on abortion practice, she seemed to take it as a matter of course. She concluded that abortion provision is simply too risky because of the violence of the antiabortion movement, which she felt could put her family at risk.

A similar concern for personal safety was voiced by Dr. Abigail Turley. Dr. Turley also identifies as pro-choice and had thought she would continue to provide abortions until she took a job in a rural western area. She said the decision not to provide abortion was partly just bad timing, as her acceptance of the job coincided with the shooting of abortion provider Dr. Barnett Slepian in Buffalo, New York, in 1998 (Yardley and Rohde 1998). "When I was interviewing for this job," she said, "it happened to be the same weekend that Slepian got killed in his kitchen. And so I, I mean, I did terminations and I thought that that might be part of my normal everyday practice because that's what I was accustomed to. But after that experience, I just said it wasn't worth it. [It's a] small town, and I didn't want to have to worry about all of that—you know, get a [bullet-proof] vest and all that." Dr. Turley and Dr. Peterson both took jobs in small, politically conservative towns where the antiabortion movement has greater purchase. This might explain why safety issues were of marked concern for them. Generally, physicians I spoke with were more vocal about stigma and political contention related to abortion and less so about their fears of violence—although the understanding of abortion work as potentially unsafe was present regardless. Interestingly, while the risk of violence to abortion providers and those they love is perceived to be greater in rural areas, in reality, more shootings have occurred in urban and suburban settings.[4] Perhaps it is the increased visibility that a smaller population provides that makes the threat of violence feel greater.

In a large eastern city, Dr. Brian Smits similarly appeared disassociated when he talked about how happy he was not to be involved with elective abortion. Dr. Smits did many abortions during training because he was subspecializing in perinatology (high-risk obstetrics). He generally receives abortion requests only for medical and genetic indications. He said, however, that he prefers it this way, largely so that he can stay above the fray of abortion politics: "I'm actually pretty happy that I don't do the elective terminations anymore . . . Maybe it's just, you know, being selfish on my part and just saying, 'Well, that's out there and let somebody else deal with it,' even though I am pro-choice, you know. And I just deal with the fetal anomalies now. It certainly makes it less complicated for me." Whether their motivation was to steer clear of controversy or potential violence, Drs. Peterson, Turley, and Smits held in common the tendency to distance themselves from personal and professional responsibility for the problem of abortion provision. For them, it is someone else's problem, and one they do not feel professionally obligated to fix.

Willing-unable physicians who expressed a desire to include abortion in their current practices but were constrained by their group or hospital policy make up a more clear-cut group. These physicians want to provide abortions, but they face seemingly insurmountable barriers to doing so. More physicians I spoke with fit into this category than into any other. Unlike physicians who disassociated themselves from the problem, these willing-unable physicians expressed regrets and felt responsible for not overcoming the barriers. They take ownership of the problem, and yet they fail to "solve" it for a variety of reasons. Because the barriers constraining the practice of these willing-unable physicians are the focus of much of this book, I provide only a few examples here in order to show how their sense of professional obligation differs from that of those physicians who disassociate themselves from the issue.

After completing his residency in a western city, Dr. John Brill continued to provide abortions in the private practice he joined there. However, he later moved to a small, semi-rural western town to be closer to his extended family and found that offering abortion in his practice would be very noticeable. "It was easier when I practiced [in the city]," he said, "because I practiced in a setting where I was with other providers who performed abortions. Some of them didn't. Some of them felt very strongly against it, but we were in a large enough group that some did, some didn't. And so if you wanted to, it was okay. Where I practice now . . . it's a small town and none of the ob-gyns perform abortions." Dr. Brill was afraid that by standing out as the lone abortion provider in town, his newly founded private practice would suffer, in part through lack of referrals from local physicians and in part by gaining a reputation as the practice of "the abortionist" in town. Yet he went on to voice his concern for how that affects patients and to express guilt about contributing to the problem of the stigmatization of abortion:

There's a couple of us that feel like—not feel like—*know that* patients aren't being cared for as well as they could be . . . not being able to be cared for by their physician . . . I've had patients who've requested abortions now and, frustratingly, I have a choice, you know. I could choose to be the rogue new physician in town who's trying to build an ob-gyn practice and who also performs abortions. And frustratingly, that would be a surefire way for me to absolutely drive my practice into the ground so that I could then take care of no one. . . .

I struggle with this a lot. It's like, what am I going to do? Am I going to just abandon these people? I can't—you can't abandon them. So that's where I scramble to find . . . the middle ground where I can refer my patients to people that are adequately trained, doing a good job, and still not provide them myself so that I can remain a member of good standing in the community. So, you know, that can be a cop-out or a good rationalization. There's a ton of different ways to look at it.

His use of the words *cop-out* and *rationalization* indicates that Dr. Brill feels professionally obligated to provide abortions and address the shortage of abortion providers in his area. He compensated for his decision, as many physicians do, by focusing on developing a referral network for his abortion patients instead of providing the abortions himself. Nevertheless, he responded to my questions about his practice with regret and discontent. Although Dr. Brill does not completely abdicate his responsibility to provide abortions, he is uncomfortable with how he has lived up to the image he had of himself as a physician earlier in his career.

Similarly, Dr. Rita Gallo is unhappy with how little involvement she has in abortion care. In her case, she completed a fellowship in family planning and abortion and had always expected abortion to be part of her practice, but she works in a large western city in an HMO that contracts out all of its abortion cases to a nearby abortion clinic. "I'm really dismayed about it," Dr. Gallo said. "And I really love my job here, but it makes me kind of sad. Because I feel like I have this skill, I should be spreading it around . . . For the first few years we used to do [abortions] on Saturdays, but there weren't very many providers who wanted to give up their Saturday morning to come and do abortions, and so I did a lot of them myself." When that became hard for Dr. Gallo's family, she stopped working Saturdays, but the program collapsed without her.

She worked to get the HMO to bring in outsiders, such as fellows from the nearby university, to staff their abortion service, but ultimately the HMO administrators decided it would be simpler to contract out to a local abortion clinic. She dislikes having to refer patients out: "I'm sure [patients are] thinking, 'Well, why doesn't [the HMO] just provide that?' You know, it seems like a simple enough thing. So, that's a political thing that I can't—I've tried to sort of go back and forth with, but so far, we're not doing very well. Anyway, it's fine, you know, it's fine. But it's not what I envisioned."

Given Dr. Gallo's dissatisfaction with the level of involvement she has had in abortion care, I asked whether she ever moonlights in the local abortion clinics. But the HMO she works for limits moonlighting. "Every [branch of our HMO] says if you have a job outside, you have to give them the money that you make from [that] job," she explained. "So I suppose I could do it, and just give them what I make, and essentially do it as a volunteer thing . . . I work full time, I mean it is kind of hard. But I could, I guess, if I wanted to. But I wouldn't be able to get paid. I guess that's what it is; I guess I haven't thought about it enough to—guess I'm not as committed as I think." Dr. Gallo's reply devolved into an internal ramble while she questioned herself as to what stops her from providing abortion outside of her job. Clearly, it is very important to her and her identity to provide the service; yet her job already demands about sixty hours per week, so, as she says, volunteering beyond that would certainly show a high degree of commitment. But given that she does not work in an area of the country with a provider shortage, she may find such a choice hard to justify to herself and her family.

Dr. Stacy Kern's involvement with abortion was limited by family matters as well. Her husband's job necessitated a move to a midsized midwestern city that has only two ob-gyn practice groups, both of which prohibit abortion. Similar to Dr. Brill and Dr. Gallo, she wonders how patients are affected by being told that they need to go elsewhere for abortion care:

> Ideally, I'd like to be in this group and have them be more permissive about [providing abortions]. So if a patient wanted that procedure done, they could get it done here and not have to go someplace that they've never been, some [doctor] they've never met and have this procedure done like it was a bad thing . . . Ideally, I would like to be able to provide

all the care my patients want. It's not my job to tell them what's right or wrong. If they make a decision on what they want to do, I feel they should be able to have the care that they need done safely, in the most efficient manner, by nonjudgmental practitioners . . . But I don't get to choose that at this point in time.

Dr. Kern is resigned to the fact that she cannot offer abortions within her current medical group, but she wonders how she might change her practice if there were no good abortion provider nearby: "If I were working here and there was nobody in town or within a reasonable radius that performed that procedure, I don't know what I would do. There's a part of me that . . . would like to think that I would try to offer that service to people in the community . . . But it just hasn't come to that yet."

These constrained physicians consistently expressed regret about their inability to offer abortions to most of their patients. They each discussed the different variables in their lives that would need to change in order for them to become an abortion provider, and perhaps someday in the future they will. One could argue that the constrained physicians differ from disassociated physicians merely in personality—the constrained being those who wrangle with already-made decisions, and the disassociated being those who do not. While it may appear superficially as such, the important difference between the two groups is that the guilt and regret of the constrained group imply dissatisfaction with the situation, a sense of personal failure in not meeting what they saw as their professional obligations, and, perhaps, a willingness to make some degree of sacrifice to include abortion in their practices (though not the current sacrifice required). In contrast, the disassociated group appears to see the need for sacrifice as reason enough to dispense with professional obligation toward abortion care. That is, "legitimate" medicine should be admirable and comfortable work, not work that requires sacrifices in prestige, professional opportunity, and personal safety.

With regard to their abortion morality and degree of politicization, constrained physicians differ little from willing-able doctors working on the front lines, the focus of the next section. They are set apart mainly by the circumstances of their practice environments and the various barriers they have encountered. These constrained physicians perceive such barriers as nearly concrete. It would take moving to a new city, giving up an otherwise ideal job, or fighting a professionally threatening battle with co-workers to change the situation. The defining aspect of constrained physicians is that while they view abortion as a professional obligation, they have geographic and professional commitments that preclude most abortion provision and (only slightly) surpass their politics in importance.

Willing-Able

Borrowing Carole Joffe's (1986) term from her ethnography of a family planning clinic, *front-line workers* in the context of this study are the physicians providing abortions regularly and for any reason. They are the willing *and* able doctors. Given that, as this book argues, most abortion providers effectively "subspecialize" in abortion care, this group represents the highest degree of professional obligation toward abortion. While several physicians from my primary sample of thirty ob-gyn graduates had some level of involvement in abortions after residency for genetic and medical indications, very few regularly did elective abortions, making this a relatively small category.

Dr. Victoria Berman is the only physician in my primary sample who at the time of the interview was successfully integrating abortion into her private-practice job. However, doing this was not without problems, even where she worked in a liberal urban area. After graduating from residency, she sought out a job that would tolerate abortion practice. "I interviewed at several places," she said, "but some of them did not do abortions and were . . . pretty conservative overall. But—I mean—I didn't want to go there anyway." Abortion was not the only political concern in her job search. She knew that she wanted to share a practice with politically "like-minded" physicians. Once she took her job, to her surprise she quickly became overwhelmed by requests for abortions:

> When I was first here, all of a sudden all these people started coming to me, who I had never met before, for an abortion. And word got out that I took [Medicaid], and so all these people . . . started coming to me out of the blue for these procedures, and at the same time new patients were coming to me—I'm in private practice and I do a general [obstetrics and] gynecology practice. People that were being referred to me for just regular

gynecological problems were having a hard time getting in because [of]
all these people [who wanted abortions], and I was doing, I don't know,
five procedures a week or something. It was a lot.

For a general ob-gyn clinic, five abortion procedures a week felt like too
many to Dr. Berman because they take longer than a typical appointment.
Furthermore, in Dr. Berman's practice, they are done off-site in a surgical
facility and necessitate help from staff members to coordinate supplies
and act as counselors to patients, and Dr. Berman's office staff reacted to
the increase negatively:

> My help here [were saying], "We're so depressed, we're doing too much
> of this" . . . And it was stressful for them . . . It's hard and I didn't want
> to turn into a Planned Parenthood here because I'd rather do lots of dif-
> ferent things in addition to [abortion]. And so what we started doing is
> . . . for my own patients who are established, I do [the abortion], and
> never a question. And I take some people who I've never met before for
> [abortions], and beyond that we end up telling them about their other
> options.

Because she herself worried that she would be unable to establish a general practice with such a high proportion of abortion patients, Dr. Berman
responded by reducing the number of such patients she would accept.
The abortion policy she created was not unique. In Dr. Brill's first job with
a practice in a large western city that had no abortion prohibition, he remembered his coworkers' concern about the same thing:

> They didn't want their practice to grow into being an abortion clinic. But
> if you had patients of your own who had an unintended pregnancy, un-
> desired pregnancy, and wanted to terminate the pregnancy, that was legit
> . . . You could take a referral from another, like, from a family practice
> doc, but what they didn't want was people calling up and saying, "Well, I
> heard Dr. Brill provides a lot of abortions and I don't have a doctor. But I
> think I'm pregnant. Can I come in and have an abortion?"

Dr. Brill's and Dr. Berman's stories exemplify what many physicians
fear about incorporating abortion into their practices. Because of the un-

even distribution of abortion provision across the profession, becoming a provider brings with it the possibility that abortion could take over a practice, replace other procedures, and in some cases upset staff members who are not supportive of abortion or simply not emotionally prepared to act as counselors for the array of psychosocial issues that accompany the procedure. Professionally, physicians worry that they will become less established and less known for their other ob-gyn skills. And politically, they worry about damage to their practices by becoming known in the community as abortion providers. Regardless of the fact that Dr. Berman, like Dr. Brill's former associates, decided to refer unknown abortion patients elsewhere, she remains a front-line physician because she successfully managed to work around the various obstacles such that she could continue to provide abortions to all of her own private-practice patients. Many physicians are more easily deterred. Doing abortions on occasion, and in the context of a known patient, has proved to be manageable in her practice.

Because the vast majority of abortion work in the United States is done in dedicated abortion clinics, other physicians I spoke with who provided abortions regularly were connected to such a service. From my primary sample of thirty, three physicians in large western cities had in the past taken fellowships in family planning during which abortion was the majority of their work. Later, after two of them, Dr. Anna Lee and Dr. Carrie Becker, became faculty physicians in the academic departments that housed their fellowships, they continued with this focus on abortion. When I asked Dr. Lee what drew her to this work she replied: "It became obvious that I had a certain comfort level that very few people have with abortion care. And so I felt that because of that interest and also because of the lack of interest from everybody else, I felt that it was important for me to go into fellowship and continue this care." Essentially, Dr. Lee viewed her comfort with abortion as a precious resource. She knew it was relatively rare and felt responsible to use it and expand on it.

Dr. Becker would probably relate to Dr. Lee's perspective. Her work has been focused on abortion and family planning for most of her career as well:

> I would say the majority of my practice is abortion and contraception care . . . now I'm the assistant director of the [family planning] fellowship, so—when I joined the faculty, I was like, "This is my area of expertise, I'm going

to continue this." And so basically I've kind of kept my generalist foot in
the door, but then because we don't do a ton of second-trimester abortions
at the university, I've contracted out to do second-trimester abortions at a
local clinic. . . I'm contracted out to do first-trimester abortions with them
at another clinic. . . we don't have an in-house abortion clinic. . . and so
they have me contracted out to do that kind of work.

Drs. Lee and Becker spend the majority of their time doing abortions,
teaching residents how to do abortions, and administering abortion services in their programs. However, their schedules are more diversified
than those of many abortion providers, who work exclusively in family
planning and abortion clinics, in that they continue to participate in other
aspects of obstetrics and gynecology through their obligations as faculty
physicians in the residency programs where they teach. In these academic
settings they enjoy relative protection from the problems that surround
abortion in the rest of the United States. In addition to the fact that these
two physicians both live in cities that many consider politically liberal, their
academic departments provide another layer of insulation from abortion
contention. The university environments and the related high status of
the fellowships make their expertise in abortion prestigious to most of the
people they interact with professionally. Worlds apart from the physicians
setting up practice in a small town (like Dr. Brill), they found the risks of
violence, stigma, and professional conflict less immediately threatening.

In the end, working on the front lines of abortion care means making abortion a high priority. Most physicians in my study ultimately
privileged location (proximity to family) over freedom from practice
restrictions when these two variables were at odds, and hence, they no
longer performed abortions. In contrast, Dr. Berman deliberately sought
a practice with a politically liberal environment in a region known to be
liberal as well and was therefore able to continue providing abortions after
residency. Dr. Lee and Dr. Becker made abortion and reproductive health
their life's work by becoming specialists in abortion care and teaching
abortion procedures to residents in university hospitals. Given the barriers to abortion practice and the stigma that surrounds it, becoming an
abortion provider does not prove to be something one stumbles upon accidentally. Rather, it is a choice and a commitment held by those who are
significantly politicized and show the highest degree of professional ob-

ligation toward abortion care, while not being strongly tied to politically conservative areas of the country, small towns, or both.

Summary

Among the physicians in this study, attitudes toward abortion practice and the extent to which they felt professionally obligated to provide abortion varied widely, regardless of the fact that the sample largely identified as pro-choice. Some unwilling physicians opted out of abortion training because of their moral convictions, and others simply saw abortion as superfluous to their professional goals. Those who became morally conflicted about providing abortion, in contrast, at times did feel responsible for providing abortion but weighed that against their discomfort with the destruction of fetal and embryonic life. Doctors who disassociated themselves from the issue of abortion altogether saw the inconveniences created by the abortion controversy as responsible for their lack of involvement and did not perceive themselves as professionally responsible to overcome them. In contrast, the willing-unable physicians often felt a great degree of responsibility and obligation to provide abortions but were unable to overcome barriers to doing so. And finally, the willing-able physicians made abortion a professional and personal priority, at times to the exclusion of other parts of ob-gyn practice.

If one were to evaluate physician willingness to provide abortions merely on the basis of the actual number they perform, the picture would be greatly skewed. My findings indicate that under less contentious political conditions and less restrictive professional circumstances, numerous physicians would practice differently. Ultimately, the lack of formalized and universal codes of professional obligation toward abortion care within medicine means that physicians (and their groups and hospitals) generally practice according to the norms of the local medical community.

The contention surrounding abortion and the related shrinking provider base put many of these physicians in a unique position. Most were aware that they possessed the skills needed to address a problem, and some felt a significant amount of professional obligation to do so. Without a clear mandate, however, physicians sifted through the perceived risks and moral dilemmas in order to explain how much involvement they were willing and able to take on. Not surprisingly, a high degree of politicization appears to be very important to physicians' ability to overcome structural obstacles to abortion practice; and still, for some, the constraints of their circumstances are too much even when they feel strongly obligated to provide abortion services to their patients.

CHAPTER 4

Dr. Anderson's Choices:
On Learning, Doing, and Having Abortions

Dr. Rina Anderson and I played phone tag for months before our interview. I planned to interview her by phone because I was unable to travel to her city. When she first returned my call, she left a message saying, "I'm thirty-six weeks pregnant, on bed rest. It's a great time for me to talk." But when I returned her call a week later, she had already had the baby. Her father answered the phone. He had a very tender voice and kindly explained that she was busy nursing and could he please leave a message for her. Kicking myself for having missed her window of bed-rest leisure (or captivity), I replied: "Yes, but this is not urgent. Please ask her to call me at her convenience."

She did not return my call. Busy doing other interviews around the country, and assuming that she was probably consumed by the adjustment to life with a newborn, I waited. Two months later I left another message. Two more months passed with no response. Then I got a message: "I'm really sorry it's taken me so long to call you back. I had a hard summer. My baby died. I still really want to participate. Please give me a call."

I was stunned, deeply saddened, and instantly grateful that she told me this information in a message (no doubt intentional). This way, she didn't have to endure what was destined to be the emotional and awkward response of a mother of two small and thankfully healthy children. I worried how she would feel about the subject matter of the interview. People who experience infertility or problem pregnancies can sometimes lose empathy for women with unwanted pregnancies. I imagined that even saying the word *abortion* might evoke pain in the context of the death of a wanted child. How would the experience of infant loss affect her comfort with abortion as a topic and a practice?

I approached our interview cautiously. I decided to make sure she took the lead on any discussion of her recent experience. When we finally connected by phone, I began as I normally would with questions about her medical background and by asking her to describe what she remembered about her experience with abortion training. I soon found out that losing this baby was not the only thing that made her story unique.

Dr. Anderson's training followed an unconventional trajectory. She initially opted out of abortion training. "At the time when I started my residency," she explained, "I had some friendship influences, some extremely strong pro-life friends from medical school." Because of this, she told her residency director she did not want abortion training. However, early in her residency she decided to opt back in. "I was always pro-choice," she said, "but I was kind of uncertain and had gotten a lot of support the other way . . . When I finally started listening to what I was thinking, then I changed my mind."

In part, her change of heart was the result of "partially" participating in the abortion rotation even though she had opted out of performing procedures; that is, she assisted on the preoperative and postoperative ends of abortion care by examining patients, gathering medical information, doing ultrasounds, filling out charts, and monitoring patient recovery. She sat in on abortion counseling sessions and learned the stories behind patients' decisions to get an abortion. Specifically, she noted that hearing the patient stories and then seeing them "move on" after the procedures changed some of her preconceptions about abortion as a potentially coercive and damaging event in women's lives. She said that just "being in the environment and seeing" the people and the process made her feel empathetic toward women getting abortions and made her want to be trained in abortion care. Dr. Anderson demonstrated ideological flexibility not often expressed around abortion. In light of this flexibility, or what one might call open-mindedness, exposure to the context of care significantly affected her training and practice choices, and ultimately her personal choices, regarding abortion.

Personal and clinical decisions do not always correlate with "pro-choice" and "pro-life" politics. Unpacking the choices that physicians such as Dr. Anderson make around learning, performing, and even having abortions serves to support an argument that observers of the medical world have made for years—that is, medicine is hardly a "hard" science (Bosk 1979; Clarke 1998; Epstein 1996; Foucault 1973; Fox 1957; Freidson 1970; Kaufman 2005; Timmermans 1999). In fact, it is enormously influenced by the proclivities of the social world. The battle cry for "evidence-based medicine" so often glosses over the politics of how (and by whom) evidence is gathered and interpreted. What physicians choose to learn, how they learn it, how they practice it, and how they apply these experiences to their own lives are complicated matters. The case of Dr. Anderson touches on all of these dimensions of abortion care and lends insight into how different health practitioners navigate their relationship to fetal life.

Abortion training, provision, and, for lack of a better word, consumption are grouped together here under the concept of choice. The word *choice* is heavily loaded in the world of abortion and has a triple meaning (at least). In both advocacy rhetoric and political forums, choice is often used synonymously with abortion itself, although it is meant to signify the "right to choose" to have one. One physician precisely and unself-consciously captured this usage while describing a colleague's somewhat ambivalent abortion philosophy: "[He felt] like, 'I believe in your choice to choose, but I don't feel comfortable with the choice to choose.'"

Still, there are elements of choice important to the discussion of abortion beyond whether to have one. Physicians can choose to get abortion training, and then later, to become a provider of abortions. Patients can choose a variety of methods to abort a pregnancy. And for a host of reasons discussed in this book, in certain cases neither physicians nor patients have much choice at all in these matters. Furthermore, some physicians make choices that seem incongruous with their abortion ideology. Thus, more often than we think, ideology and practice are separated by both structural constraints and the unique circumstances and preferences of individuals.

Partial Participation

Long before they leave residency, ob-gyn physicians, like Dr. Anderson, have a series of decisions to make concerning what they learn about abortion care. As medical students, they may need to decide whether to observe abortions during their third and fourth years, if their program provides that option. Then they need to choose a residency program, some of which offer abortion training and some of which do not. If the chosen residency program has routine (as opposed to elective) abortion training, physicians can decide to opt out of that training when they have religious or moral objections to performing abortions. If they do choose to opt out, in some programs they can decide whether to participate partially in the abortion training—partaking of teaching lectures, observing the context of care, and assisting with patients in ways other than doing procedures.[1] Even within the limited realm of partial participation, physicians must choose what their boundaries around abortion care will be and what particular tasks they are comfortable doing.

The directors of Dr. Anderson's residency program decided to formalize the opt-out process in the late 1990s. Hers was the only program of the four I studied that had (at the time) created such a formal procedure. Residents were required to present in writing and in person their moral or personal objection to abortion to a board of three attending physicians. Dr. Carrie Becker, on faculty there, explained that the procedure had two major purposes: to establish abortion training as a routine expectation of the residency and to provide a forum for values clarification.

> It's more to make sure that folks don't have misconceptions about abortion care, that they've thought about it, that they know what their limits are, if they have any questions, if we can help them learn more about themselves from it . . . And it's also to make sure that people aren't coming in and being like, "I just don't want to have to do it because it's icky." It's either religious reasons or personal moral reasons, "I don't feel like this is appropriate for me," and why. Or, "I'm totally fine with being involved in starting something but not finishing it" . . . And so what components are you comfortable with? . . . We want to make sure that we're not putting the patient and the resident in an awkward situation where they would both be uncomfortable . . . It's important to know where people's boundaries are. So that's what the opt-out board is for.

The system is little used, and Dr. Becker remembers only one physician formally opting out in the five years she was on the faculty. Because this particular residency program makes abortion training such a high priority, it undoubtedly attracts doctors who are more (rather than less) comfortable with abortion. Another graduate from Dr. Anderson's program was in residency when the opt-out procedure was established. He remembers that some observers feared that the board would intimidate residents with opposition to abortion. However, he saw the major function of the board as making it more difficult for physicians with no ideological objection to avoid the abortion training because it is less pleasant or prestigious than other activities the resident could be doing.

> Our program was very clear about the fact that [there are] a lot of things in ob-gyn that are uncomfortable and you can't opt out of something because it's unpleasant.[2] But if you need to opt out of something on strong moral grounds, that's okay. And so it was always understood that this was an expected part of your training and if you didn't want to do it, you could opt out, but basically you had to present your case . . . Initially, some people voiced some concern that that was going to be coercive, but it ended up not being that way . . . It was just to sort of clarify how you felt and to make it all shipshape. But nobody was coerced back into doing abortion training if they didn't want to.

Residencies that formalize their opt-out process in this way are rare. Whether through a panel or simply by discussing the decision to opt out with residency directors, this decision point can be an opportunity for residents to clarify what the limits of their participation might be and why. Ultimately, by making "staying in" the default status rather than "opting out," the residency directors hope to produce as many trained abortion providers as possible in order to help ameliorate the shortage of abortion providers beyond the confines of their well-served liberal city. Dr. Anderson's residency created additional legitimacy around abortion training by integrating abortion into the residents' ob-gyn clinics, where they would learn to do procedures intermingled with other office visits. Dr. Becker expressly hoped this would encourage doctors to integrate abortion into their practices in this way after graduation. While the three other programs I studied were also selected for their routine abortion training history, their cultures of practice were relatively less bold in directly endeavoring to normalize abortion practice.

Like Dr. Anderson, Dr. Francine Gray and Dr. Dan Hayner partially participated in their abortion training rotations. They both opted out of performing abortions because of their strongly held religious beliefs, but they left with divergent views on the value of this type of exposure to abortion care. Dr. Gray's residency program in the South had a lot of trouble staffing the abortion clinic during her training. At that time, the department did not prioritize teaching and curriculum development for the abortion service (this has since changed). It was what physicians commonly refer to as the "see one, do one, teach one" model of training. The teacher in this case was not necessarily an attending physician, but rather a senior-level resident, and the abortion clinic was mostly run by residents.

In Dr. Gray's program, about half of the residents typically opted out of abortion training—unlike the other three programs I studied in which opting out was rare. But in Dr. Gray's cohort, only two of the ten incoming residents went through abortion training. At one point she became aware that they were shorthanded in the abortion clinic, and she was indirectly encouraged to help out to relieve the pressure on her co-residents:

> No [faculty] ever said anything. It was more passed down through the residents: "You guys should feel bad that you're not helping out. The poor two other people are getting beat up all the time, and you guys should help them out . . ."
>
> I could see it was a problem getting enough residents to help staff the pre-op patients. So I said: "You know what? Fine. These women have made their decision. I'm not counseling them about it. I'm just going to make sure that they're safe to undergo the procedure. I'll pre-op them, but I won't consent them [do the paperwork and counseling needed to obtain patient consent for the treatment]. So the resident that's doing the procedure can consent them that day or whatever." But I said that I'll be happy to go through their medical history, their allergies, all that stuff.

Dr. Gray does not believe abortion should be illegal, yet given her Catholic identification and beliefs, she was clear that she did not want to have any involvement in the decision to abort or the actual procedure that would terminate the pregnancy. However, her boundaries became difficult to maintain when the resident who usually did consents and procedures one day failed to show up:

> It backfired on me. I still remember there was a day that they put me there by myself with no other resident—it was usually two. And I said, "Look, fine, I'll do the pre-ops." And it was really full; there were a lot of patients to be seen, and I said, "I'll see them, but I'm not going to consent them." And I had a [senior resident] who was just not a very nice individual to begin with, who absolutely lit into me about how I had to do this. And I was like, "No, I really don't have to do this" . . . I was trying to help out, and it was actually a worse situation than if I had just been adamant like some of the other people in my class that wanted absolutely nothing to do with it . . .
>
> Somebody finally did come help me. It wasn't the resident that was supposed to be there—and [that person] felt horrible that they didn't show up. But they didn't realize they were supposed to be there that day . . .
>
> It was never an attending [physician] that [admonished me for not consenting abortion patients]. It was another resident who just had her own opinions [about abortion]. See, she *did* do abortions. So she just felt obligated to stick it to me, so to speak . . . I was in bad shape that day. I do remember sitting there crying about it and getting upset.

Dr. Gray felt that her senior resident took advantage of her goodwill to help out and was insensitive, if not downright antagonistic, regarding her abortion beliefs. This was the only such altercation I heard about, and it may simply be a case of a "power-tripping" senior resident—an enduring archetype of the residency experience. However, Dr. Gray's experience demonstrates the difficulty of having to maintain boundaries around the care one will provide when care is in short supply. It was difficult for Dr. Gray to be working in a situation where she had to repeatedly assert that she would not fill particular needs—in this case obtaining patients' consent for abortion—because of her beliefs. Dr. Gray went on to work in a Catholic-owned hospital, and her professional world rarely has any involvement with abortion now except in certain cases of miscarriage management and fatal fetal anomaly.[3]

Dr. Hayner, the third physician who partially participated in abortion training, had a much more positive experience than Dr. Gray. His residency's abortion clinic was well staffed by attending physicians. Most of the residents in his program wanted abortion training, so there was no resident shortage. While Dr. Hayner believed that abortion was morally wrong and wanted no part in performing one, he reserved his disapproval for the abortion, not the patient. "I always had heard, 'love the person, dislike the act,'" he explained. "I might not necessarily agree with their choice that they're [making], but I honestly care for my patients." Similarly, he did not demonize his abortion-providing teachers, and he felt his beliefs were respected and not impinged upon. In fact, one of the most positive things he remembers about the experience was the respect that his mentors showed him regarding his personal beliefs about abortion: "I remember having kind of a long conversation with the residency director about 'OK, where do you say life starts, at what stage?' And you know, we had different views, but the thing I liked was there was no real condemnation on anybody's part, pro or against. And I think that was very helpful."

Initially, Dr. Hayner was reluctant to participate in the training because of his religious faith and personal convictions. Neither of these fundamentally changed after his rotation in the clinic, but something more subtle did. He described the kind of involvement he had in the clinic and what he learned during his rotation there:

> [We learned] how to clinically size the uterus, check for villi and stuff [to make sure the abortion was complete],[4] and a lot of those skills are things that I use in my day-to-day practice. [I] helped with the counseling. I helped, hopefully, alleviate people's fears and counsel them about the procedure, and then helped them get on an alternative form of contraception afterward. If you chose not to do the procedure, you helped up to the point of doing it and then checking the tissue [and] talking to the patient afterwards.

Dr. Hayner came to see abortion patients as more diverse than he had originally thought, indicating that he was able to relate to them as individuals and their particular life circumstances. They did not seem ignorant or immoral, as he had been taught. He was struck by his misconceptions about both abortion patients and abortion practice. "The biggest thing was seeing the broad spectrum of individuals who came requesting that service," he said. "And then the steps that were taken to say, 'This is a choice, this isn't the *only* choice' . . . I felt they could walk away." He was pleased to see that patients were not coerced into having abortions. Before he started the rotation he believed that people involved in abortion care would be more dogmatic than he found them to be. Dr. Hayner was surprised by the open-mindedness and caring he witnessed—to a great extent because it ran counter to the antiabortion imagery with which he had grown up:

> I think the empathy for the pain that people were going through both physically and emotionally . . . That was something that the nursing staff, the physician staff, very much were aware of, and [they] stepped up to meet those emotional needs . . . It's something that I think allows you to walk away from the experience feeling like, "OK, this is a worthwhile part of training." And not something that I would (A) choose to do again or (B) choose to incorporate into my practice. But, it totally opened my eyes up to the inside workings of an abortion clinic, what truly is going on. Instead of being in ignorant opposition to it, I can say I've been there, lived the experience. It's not something I'd want to do or choose for myself. But there is some respect for humanity going on inside those walls. It's not as diabolical as it seems to an outside observer.

In addition to dispelling Dr. Hayner's stereotypes around abortion, the experience of partial training influenced his practice style as well, mostly in relation to making referrals for abortions. How referrals are made is another important choice in the physician trajectory vis-à-vis abortion. Some physicians who are not sympathetic to women seeking abortions, or prefer to distance themselves from the issue, do not give referrals to abortion services and see such referrals as outside their scope of practice (Curlin et al. 2007), just as Dr. Sacks from Chapter 3 mentioned cavalierly that he sends patients who seek abortion to the phone book. Those strongly opposed to abortion argue that referrals make physicians complicit in the abortion (Chervenak and McCullough 2008). Interestingly, while both Dr. Sacks and Dr. Gray trained in the same residency program, it was Dr. Sacks who participated in abortion training. However, he was unhappy about his experience and particularly bothered by the lack of guidance on psychosocial issues. "It was handled as if it would be a usual procedure," he noted, "like delivering a baby, doing a C-section, doing a hysterectomy, tying somebody's tubes, and so on. And I think it's not the usual proce-dure. There are lots of emotional and moral issues that are involved in it." The lack of didactics addressing abortion beyond the technical training may have contributed to Dr. Sacks's lack of interest in and empathy for abortion. By choosing to refer his current patients to the telephone direc-tory when they need an abortion, Dr. Sacks sends them out without an introduction to a new provider and without a physician advocate follow-ing their care. His lack of referral also puts them at high risk of responding to misleading ads from crisis pregnancy centers throughout the United States that are funded by antiabortion groups—and while George W. Bush was in office, the federal government (Spillar 2009)—to dissuade women from getting an abortion.

Dr. Hayner, in contrast to Dr. Sacks, treats abortion referrals as similar to other procedures referred to specialists. He makes referrals to known providers and follows up on patients' care:

> I always see my own patients back [in my office after the procedure for fol-low-up]. Just because I don't do the procedure doesn't mean I don't con-tinue the relationship . . . But the knowing, having seen the experience in [residency], I have a feeling of what an empathetic environment should be for that. And I definitely have patients who come back and overall it was an okay thing, and others who are like, "I'm so glad to be back here because it was the world's worst thing, I felt like just a nobody . . . "
>
> I think that's how I've kind of weeded through [the bad providers and found good ones], and I have relationships with those providers too. In most cases, I'm calling them up and saying, "Hey, Peggy Sue or Mrs. Jones is coming to see you and this is her story." And I think that very much helps because it humanizes it for them too. And I think that is probably the key thing, is to keep the human in the process.

Ultimately, Dr. Hayner's partial participation in the abortion training pro-gram altered his perspective. That Dr. Hayner's abortion clinic was well staffed was likely influential in making his experience positive. In particu-lar, he felt it helped him clarify his own boundaries and values around abortion care. He remembers feeling that the rotation was too long at the time, but reflecting back he said, "I think ten years out, I can look at it and say, 'Oh, it is the right amount of time, and right amount of exposure.'"

Dr. Hayner also specifically noted that he appreciated that his program set aside time and space early in training for a formal abortion rotation so that he was able to clarify his feelings: "I'm glad it was early my internship year, because I was able to truly come to a grasp with it, know where I stood with it. I think that's a good thing instead of trying to subversively train people in it. Having it as a formal part of your training very much helped. Because I think if you water it down, I think it doesn't have the same impact as having it as a formal part of my training had for me." His words "water it down" referred to how some programs with no formal abortion training component provide exposure to abortion intermittently throughout the four years of residency. He explained that he had heard from colleagues about training situations in which the resident was unwittingly sent to the operating room to find out from the attending physician there that, "Oh by the way, we're going to be doing a suction D&C because [the patient] really doesn't want to be pregnant." Dr. Hayner continued: "I think that would be a lot harder to face. In that scenario, you're almost—your hands are almost tied—that they're almost forcing you to do the procedure." The power differential between an attending physician and a resident makes it difficult for the resident to say no in this setting. Such a setup may be typical for other surgeries, but for abortion Dr. Hayner (like Dr. Sacks) thinks it is important that residents are psychologically prepared to deal with the social issues surrounding abortion, that they have both the time and authority necessary to decide what their personal boundaries are around participation in abortion care, and that they are exposed to preabortion counseling so they come to know the context of patients' lives and their abortion decisions.

Dr. Hayner is still opposed to abortion on moral grounds after training, but through his exposure to abortion care, he gained compassion for the reasons why people get them and provide them. Dr. Hayner's experience is an example of how understanding context can facilitate feelings of empathy; seeing abortion care in practice can encourage physicians to relate to the patients, become less "absolutist" in their philosophy about abortion, and even increase their sense of professional obligation to refer and follow up on abortion care.

Drs. Anderson, Gray, and Hayner are three unique individuals who opted out of abortion training in three distinct residency programs. They demonstrate different responses to being "encouraged" to partially participate in abortion training when opposed to abortion in principle. For Dr. Anderson, that exposure changed her outlook entirely. Without it, she might not have ultimately become an abortion provider. Dr. Gray's outlook wasn't changed at all, and she regarded her little bit of exposure to abortion care as a wholly negative event. Dr. Hayner found empathy for those seeking and providing abortions, which influenced him to develop referral relationships with physicians he felt provided quality care and to follow up with his patients after the procedure.

Technical Expertise

Interestingly, Dr. Anderson's decision to go back and get trained to do abortions after initially opting out was not entirely grounded in her exposure to abortion care. In fact, she described the decision as partly motivated by "selfishness." "I felt like I wasn't getting enough experience doing procedures, and [I was not] feeling that comfortable with the uterus," she explained. "So selfishly, I thought if I start doing *that* I'm going to feel a lot more comfortable." To her, the desire to improve her intrauterine surgical skills seemed self-centered in contrast to presumably more altruistic concerns around destigmatizing and improving access to abortion care.

Abortion training has increased substantially for residents in U.S. obgyn residencies since the early 1990s, when it was at a postlegalization low (Eastwood et al. 2006; MacKay and MacKay 1995). More residency programs have come to consider the development of surgical competency in abortion care a professional obligation in the field. Nevertheless, Dr. Anderson's association of abortion work with altruism is not unfounded. As we have already seen, regardless of the fact that it is one of the most common ob-gyn procedures, the intense stigma and contention surrounding abortion have long marginalized the practice and the physicians who provide it. Those willing to tolerate the challenges of abortion work are often motivated by abortion politics and a concern for personal freedom, social justice, and/or public health. Because the abortion curriculum was known to be a strong part of Dr. Anderson's residency program, during her second year she went back to get exposure to lectures and training she had missed the first year. Then she proceeded, like the other residents, to provide abortions to patients throughout the remainder of her four-year program. When I asked what she found valuable about the training, she emphasized both the surgical and psychosocial skills required in abortion care: "The surgical and technical skills are very important, and then knowing how to manage complications, which you don't get that often, but you should be able to do that . . . Those are probably the most important things. And I think, even though we didn't do it as much, counseling patients and learning how to do the informed consent and discussion with them and actual counseling." However, some physicians, like Dr. Gray, who opted out of abortion training, take issue with the claim that abortion training is necessary for ob-gyns. After all, abortion requires the same technical procedure as miscarriage management. Is it not sufficient to learn to empty out the uterus on miscarriage patients? Dr. Gray contended: "It was one of the things they tried to sell to us . . . 'You would get even better at D&Cs if you had done these things' . . . And I was like, 'No, I really just don't think it's that hard of a procedure, and I've done an awful lot of [miscarriage] D&Cs to feel comfortable.' I mean, maybe in certain programs where the numbers [of patients to learn on] were lower, but our numbers for that kind of stuff were fine." Dr. Gray's opinion holds more weight for first-trimester than for second-trimester procedures. Abortions during the first trimester are relatively safe and simple procedures, as are miscarriage completions that mostly occur in the first trimester. Second-trimester surgical abortions and miscarriage completions (dilation and evacuation, D&E) have higher rates of complication and necessitate substantial training (Grimes 2008; Grimes and Schulz 1985).

Complication management was a particularly important benefit of training for several of the physicians I spoke with, because uterine perforations can go unnoticed by the physician and bleeding can escalate quickly. These problems can occur in other surgeries related to the uterus. Physicians who had a lot of abortion training, especially in the second trimester, talked about the confidence they gained from seeing and managing the complications that arose. Dr. Rebecca Holmes, who trained at a program in the Northeast with a high daily abortion patient load, especially in the second trimester, did not enjoy the experience very much. In fact, she remembered wishing she could opt out but didn't feel entitled to do so because she did not have religious objections to abortion. "If you had religious beliefs," she said, "you could get out of doing them . . . So of course everyone's trying to do that because it was scut work anyway."[5] She found the early abortion work monotonous and second-trimester abortions visually and emotionally disturbing. In addition to having the highest patient load, her residency's abortion training was longer in duration than the other programs in the study. Looking back, however, she came to value the surgical skills she developed there:

> [Abortions] used to scare the living daylights out of me because there were so many complications that could happen . . . I always felt like, "Oh, God," what if you [perforate the uterus]? I remember doing the D&Cs [to complete] the second trimesters [inductions], and you could just feel the uterus was [soft and easy to perforate] . . . [but doing] it was really good because it gave me that experience of getting in once a week and having to scrape out these boggy uteruses . . . and get used to [asking myself], "Okay, it's bleeding and how am I going to stop it?" And that is something I really drew on as an attending [physician] . . . And I actually did not appreciate it at the time . . . I assumed everyone had that kind of training . . . and I watched one of my colleagues—who didn't get the same training I got—not handle that as well. [That person] ran into more complications. That's truly when I began to say, "You know what, that training was extremely valuable."

Physicians like Dr. Holmes who did numerous (I estimate between twenty-five and seventy-five) late-second-trimester abortions during training came to appreciate the superiority of their skills when they saw the results of less-skilled abortion care. Only 27 percent of ob-gyns from residencies with routine abortion training (17 percent from residencies with elective abortion training) performed more than ten such procedures during training (Eastwood et al. 2006). Dr. Holmes had exceptional intrauterine surgical skills. Because of this, most ob-gyns with less training refer patients requiring second-trimester surgical abortion procedures (even when they do not have moral objections) to physicians with training at the level of Dr. Holmes. In emergency cases, though, one hopes to have a physician with good second-trimester training nearby.

Dr. Sarah Thompson, a physician from my supplementary sample who did a fellowship in family planning and abortion care, shared two stories of emergency care when her second-trimester abortion skills proved to be critical. In the first, she recalled managing serious complications caused by an abortion provider with poor surgical skills in her midwestern town:

> There was a guy who . . . had a clinic where it [the abortion] was a hundred dollars, so a cheaper alternative to Planned Parenthood. And they were almost all illegal immigrants that went there [from the] farms and the meat-packing industry. Tons of migrant workers. [We had] two very bad complications from his clinic . . . I don't know what his training was, nor his medical ethics. He dropped a patient off at the emergency department who was hemorrhaging, with a note saying what he'd done. She's lucky to [be alive]. He perforated out through the uterine artery and, you know, she was twenty-one [years old]. They called me to the ER because they knew that I knew the most about abortions in the hospital . . . Fortunately, we were able to save her uterus. I've learned some tricks from some of the older guys[6] . . . So I've seen several [complications]. They're pretty bad, and I don't know how many [women] had problems that didn't come in.

Another emergency case where her training was critical came up in the last four minutes of the interview when I asked, "How would you summarize what being trained in abortion adds to your practice or your repertoire, who you are?" She responded with the following story:

> This is maybe the best way to kind of sum it up. We had this patient who I was consulted on [when I worked in the Midwest] who was twenty-three or twenty-four weeks [pregnant] who'd had ruptured membranes for several days, was clearly septic and sick.[7] And the baby was still alive. And so her husband would not permit her to have an abortion because it was an abortion.
>
> He finally consented to an induction—but the doses [of labor-inducing medications] had to be far lower so it wouldn't distress the baby. And it's like, "Okay, now your wife is dying, she's dying, hello!" And at this point she was too ill to [continue laboring]—she was septic. And so finally the perinatologist convinced him that she should have the abortion.
>
> And I went up and I met him. He treated me just like dirt, like I was the garbage cleaner. And I'm like: "You know, your wife might die and I think I have maybe a 10 percent or 20 percent chance of perforating her

uterus. She's septic, it's just all going to be mush . . . this would have been better if I had done this three days ago . . ." So we do the procedure, it goes completely uncomplicated. I didn't even lose a drop of blood, clearly just fine. And the first thing he asked—not how is his wife—[but rather] can he see the fetus.

Dr. Thompson was angered by the husband's lack of respect for her as a physician, but his lack of concern for his wife's health in comparison to that of the fetus particularly infuriated her. In obstetrics, the pregnant woman, not the fetus, is the patient, and when their interests are at odds with one another, ob-gyns are largely trained to put the woman's interests first. Yet because the patient was unable to provide consent for herself, her husband had power over the course of care, and the physicians were forced to defer to him. Dr. Thompson went on:

Anyway, his wife did great. And she got pregnant again, and she picked me as her obstetrician, which I was really surprised about. And she's like, "Well, you clearly were a great doctor." And her husband treated me so rude through the whole pregnancy. And at the end I said to him, because he had an issue with going to an abortion provider, "You know, the only reason I was able to save your wife's life was because I had the skills that I learned [by] doing abortions . . . that's the only way I could get the volume to [have] this skill . . . if I had never done a bunch of late-term abortions, I probably would have killed your wife, or she would have had to have a hysterectomy, that would have been it, and she would have been lucky to survive that, being [as sick as] she was." And he didn't get it, but she really did.

Because abortion training is such an efficient way to acquire the skills to safely manage second-trimester pregnancy loss, some residencies deliberately assign patients with the least controversial indications (that is, fetal anomalies, maternal health problems, or fetal demise) to residents who have opted out of abortion training so that they can have some exposure and develop these skills, albeit in a more limited way. For example, Dr. Becker said, "If there was an anomaly, we tried to funnel that person in there . . . so that they would actually still get the experience to do those procedures, because they're important procedures to do because they teach you all sorts of other things as well." In the absence of a skilled provider, physicians with limited experience during training might suffice in an emergency. As with most surgeries, however, doctors who have performed more abortions during training, and who maintain those skills after residency, are known to have better safety records than those who do not have that training and experience.

Moral Meanings and Motives

Developing technical skills is only part of abortion training. Also important is training in the psychological aspects of getting and performing abortions, which means being prepared to take an active role in an emotionally, politically, and, for some, spiritually charged event. Abortion training is the place where doctors can develop bedside competency vis-à-vis abortion in different ways. They can develop counseling skills to help patients both with the decision to abort and with what to expect physically and psychologically if they choose to abort. Physicians also come to understand their own emotional reactions to performing abortions, especially in relation to second-trimester procedures, when they must contend with a larger fetus. A few abortion training programs have a "values clarification" curriculum, where residents can process their feelings about abortion before or throughout the training in a group or classroom setting so as to best identify their boundaries around participation and gestational age limits. Much like the concerns of the opt-out board that Dr. Becker articulated above, this curriculum seeks to create a forum for residents to discuss political, moral, and emotional challenges in abortion work and in doing so learn to recognize their feelings and judgments so that such feelings do not unexpectedly surface in an unprofessional way while the residents are interacting with abortion patients. Ideally, after creating this awareness, residents can modify their behavior, if necessary, in order to treat patients with respect.

When physicians do not "feel" respectful, it remains a professional duty to treat patients with respect anyway. This comportment, a job requirement that Arlie Hochschild (1985) termed *emotion work*, can be particularly challenging to sustain when physicians lack empathy for abortion patients. Hochschild showed that when people are professionally obligated to display emotions that they do not feel, they experience a kind of alienation from self, as did the flight attendants in her study who became tired of wearing a smile for rude passengers. "Faking it," or what she calls *surface acting*, is hard to maintain over long periods, whereas invoking feelings of empathy, or what she calls *deep acting*, is more sustainable. For example, the flight attendants would perform the mental exercise of imagining their passengers were small children in order to facilitate empathy for their demanding behavior. Similarly, physicians who feel empathetic about the issues surrounding abortion in general are more capable of deep acting when necessary—in this case, sustaining a compassionate and sensitive demeanor toward particular patients whose behavior physicians judge negatively. In theory, by clarifying what judgments they have toward abortion patients, physicians can better know the specific challenges to their ability to sustain respectful care.

I was curious to know how Dr. Anderson reacted emotionally to learning how to perform abortions, given her initial decision to opt out and the antiabortion influences in her life. She explained that the first-trimester experiences were "totally fine." But, she continued, "I think when we did the second-trimesters and learned D&Es and such, that's always harder . . . in the same [time period] you're doing rotations in [extremely premature obstetrics] where you're . . . giving meds to these babies and trying to save them . . . But really, I didn't have any bad experiences . . . It was disturbing at first doing them, but I actually, I think I was able to kind of detach a little bit too, emotionally." Like most physicians I have spoken with, Dr. Anderson made a qualitative distinction between first-trimester and second-trimester abortions. According to CDC data from 2003, second-trimester abortions constitute roughly 11 percent of all abortion procedures, a proportion that has stayed constant since 1983 even as the total number of abortions has slightly ebbed and flowed (Strauss et al. 2006). For residents, it can be a difficult balance to learn to do second-trimester abortions on fetuses that are sometimes only weeks or days younger than the premature babies they are learning to save in another part of the hospital. Early abortions reveal very little recognizable tissue, and therefore the moral questions tend to hover around sexual morality and the abstract conceptualization of personhood (that is, what is "acceptable" sexual and reproductive behavior for women?

How "human" is an embryo or fetus? Is killing the embryo or fetus wrong?). On the other hand, fetuses past thirteen or fourteen weeks look more "babylike," and that resemblance can present moral challenges to even the most politically motivated pro-choice physicians who do not find first-trimester abortion problematic. Therefore, added to the anti-abortion imagery of dismembered fetuses from protesters and the media, residents incorporate first-hand imagery of neonatal intensive care patients and their anguished parents. This gives many residents pause. Physicians who become comfortable performing second-trimester abortions (D&Es) do often learn, as Dr. Anderson says, "to detach" from the process (Lief and Fox 1963; Parsons 1951; Smith and Kleinman 1989).[8]

But if they "detach" from the physicality of abortion, they seem to "attach" themselves to the woman and her situation. At the very core of abortion work is the value that abortion is a personal choice that should not be judged or evaluated by anyone other than the pregnant woman herself, but the justification for the abortion nevertheless seems to remain important in the hearts and minds of providers. In order to justify it, many seek to understand why patients choose it. Some have called this the *ethics of care* (Gilligan 1982), where an ethical problem moves from being abstract and faceless to being concrete and intimate. A physician's concern for the welfare of real people in difficult situations can engender empathy for patient choices even when ethical principles are breached. During research for my ethnography of an abortion clinic in 2000, a resident who had recently completed her training (which included a majority of second-trimester abortion procedures) told me how learning about patients' life circumstances was more disturbing to her than learning to dismember fetuses:

> So what was emotional for me about the rotation was the women and their stories. Like the week when I did two thirteen-year-olds' twenty-three-week abortions, and then I had the woman who was suicidal and we had to get her . . . admitted [into the hospital] and didn't do her abortion that day. And then the woman who had gone to [the Crisis Pregnancy Center] and they told her she wasn't pregnant at twelve weeks and totally lied, and then she actually came to us too late to have an abortion, like three months later. She was sixteen years old . . . And that was the week that the woman drove [eight hours] because no one in [her state] would

do her abortion . . . So it wasn't the *body parts* that were freaking me out, it was just the *heaviness of these women's lives.*

In sympathizing with their patients' predicaments, physicians can feel their work is meaningful and worthwhile. Second-trimester abortion has lower public approval than first-trimester abortion because of beliefs that more developed fetuses are more "human," as well as the tendency to judge women as irresponsible for "waiting" to abort. Physicians who resist such judgment are motivated to persevere in the face of the disturbing physicality of later-gestation abortions in several ways. They often ground their motives broadly in the ethics of personal freedom (the right of the patient to make decisions pertaining to her body), social justice (how lack of reproductive control can increase existing economic and health disparities), and/or public health (the morbidity and mortality caused by unsafe or illegal abortion).

In daily practice, physicians use certain mechanisms and narratives to remind themselves of these motives. One way this is done in the context of patient care is by *identifying with the patient's story,* or in essence, putting themselves in the patient's shoes. Again, during my ethnographic research of 2000, the residency director told me that he maintained his empathy for patients by asking them directly about the circumstances of their lives:

> I suppose seeing all of the situations that occur, talking to more and more patients about how they happen to be in this situation, which I always do [now]—I didn't used to always. Now, I feel more comfortable. I didn't want to appear judgmental by saying, "Well, how did you ever get into this mess?" but now I ask them, and when somebody tells you something, you understand the situation better, even if you might have done it a different way yourself. . .
>
> I tell the residents, "Just ask about it, you'll be sympathetic." Even the students who are there for such a short time, if they would really find out the women's stories, they would be sympathetic. . . I don't think they feel as comfortable because they haven't been at it as long, you know, asking somebody from the jail, "How did you end up in jail?"

Often, physicians do not have as much time or opportunity to chat with patients, so they read the counseling notes or talk directly to the counselor to find out what motivated the decision to abort. Therefore, in these cases they know going into the operating room some of the social issues around the abortion. If physicians can empathize, it helps them see the procedure as more necessary and helpful than destructive. For example, physicians empathized easily with women who were raped or who had fetal anomalies and did not want to continue the pregnancy for such reasons. Physicians also tended to sympathize with issues of poverty and lack of control in patients' lives. For example, one physician in the South, recalling her experience with residency abortion training, explained:

> There were many patients who said, "I'm barely making ends meet with two children, can't afford this one, it's not fair to the child" . . . It broke my heart sometimes, knowing that they were doing something that a lot of people turn their nose up at, or thought was morally wrong, and these women had struggled, and they made a decision that many times was handling their life situation as best they could. And actually not thinking about themselves, but thinking about how [the pregnancy] would impact [their family] and not be fair to the child they'd be bringing into this world.

In the absence of an empathetic story, it seemed that doctors would focus on the general desire for wanted and healthy babies in the world. This is the perspective of *every child a wanted child*. Patients having second-trimester (especially late-second-trimester) abortions are not infrequently drug users, victims of rape and incest, teenagers in denial, or mentally ill women. Having seen babies born to such patients on the labor and delivery ward, some physicians find motivation in helping women stop the destructive cycle (a woman's life feels out of control, she gets pregnant, she has children whose lives also end up out of control because of a lack of good parenting and resources, the children get pregnant, and so on). Dr. Holmes captured this sentiment when she explained her feelings around performing second-trimester procedures, whether they are for miscarriage or elective abortion:

> If it's [a miscarriage], you are like [*with a pained voice*], "Oh, here's this little life!" And you know that it was meant to be because, that's what happened. And if it's an abortion, you just feel sad that the woman wasn't

able to raise the child. But I totally respect the decision, having seen—The thing about [residency] is you did see all the abuse. You see the kids that ended up in the NICU [neonatal intensive care unit] just waiting to get picked up by [social services] . . . you saw enough of the other end, like people walking in, abrupting on coke with no prenatal care,[9] that you're like, "Oh my God, it's like you took this child and took them from the starting line and made them go back and run." It's like they're never going to even make it to the starting line of life.

Dr. Holmes finds it unpleasant doing abortions in general, but when doing them she would at times evoke the memory of these drug-addicted women giving birth to drug-addicted children who would be taken into custody immediately and have a very precarious beginning in life. Perhaps, in her case, the fact that Dr. Holmes did not continue providing abortions speaks to the limitations of evoking this memory for motivation—one could argue that many aborted babies would have been adopted and wanted by loving parents. However, doctors generally did not mention adoption as a meaningful alternative, largely because the adoption rate is less than 1 percent of all unintended pregnancies, whereas abortion accounts for 50 percent of unintended pregnancies (Atwood 2007; Guttmacher Institute 2006; Richards 2007). Even when the pregnancy is unwanted and finances are tight, women who do not abort tend to want to keep their babies.

Another empathy-generating tool that has motivated many doctors for years to continue to perform abortions at all legal gestations is the *public health narrative*, which holds that abortion is, and has always been, a reality; women who want abortions will get them somehow; and it is a physician's duty to ensure that abortions are safe. This narrative has been an especially strong motivator for physicians who practiced before *Roe*, such as Dr. Chasey, featured in the introduction of the book. Independent of moral questions around abortion, many physicians feel it is their professional obligation to make abortion safe and accessible in order to prevent the maternal deaths and damage witnessed before legalization, and which endure in many other countries today where abortion is illegal and unsafe. Dr. Thompson captured the spirit of this outlook when she said: "If every single pregnancy was wanted and nobody ever ruptured their membranes at twenty-three weeks and I never had to do this, I'd be super happy, couldn't be happier. Great. People shouldn't have surgeries if they don't need them. But that's not how we live."

Doctors can hold all these perspectives at the same time, and often they do. Some individuals form a *composite woman-centered narrative* such that they stop looking at counseling notes, or don't need to. For example, the head nurse who managed pain medication for patients in the abortion clinic I studied in 2000 explained that before going into the operating room, she usually liked to read counselors' notes, but if she didn't, she said, "It's the same, it's like a general concept that this woman is here for an abortion because she is not ready to have the baby, and she has plans for herself, and just be there for her support. But I wouldn't know that she was abused and this and all that, the special things on the patient. I wouldn't know that if nobody tells me or I don't see the chart. It's still the same." Thus, she likes to have the information about patients' lives in order to connect with patients and empathize, but if there is no time or opportunity to read the notes, she has a basic narrative about why women seek abortion that she can empathize with. Along these lines, Dr. Qui Qan Wong, who trained in the Northeast, explained how initially her sympathy for the decision to abort differed with different patients, but over time, after seeing numerous women in difficult situations, she grew to generally support women's decisions independent of the individual patient context: "I think by having such a huge volume, that you get to see all aspects, [and you start simply] supporting people to have that right."

Abortion Methods in the Second Trimester

Until the 1980s, second-trimester abortions were primarily done by induction of labor and not surgical methods (D&E) because physicians believed surgical abortion beyond the first trimester was too dangerous. But a number of social factors explain why this trend continued long after D&Es were demonstrated through research to be safer than induction of labor (Grimes and Schulz 1985). Because abortion is marginalized in American medicine, technical training did not advance as quickly as it typically does in other fields. Abortion methods were not welcome topics in national medical meetings, and abortion providers often worked in isolation from each other (Joffe 1995). Without training opportunities for providing second-trimester abortions, many abortion providers tended to continue doing what they knew best through the 1980s and 1990s, and this holds true today in certain parts of the country where physicians have been slow to adopt "evidence-based" methods in abortion care.[10] Dr. Thompson explains that, certainly, in the absence of providers with strong training in second-trimester surgical abortion, induction of labor is the best choice: "It's much better for somebody to have an induction if they don't have a skilled provider. I think that there are lots of doctors that offer that to patients because they're not skilled with a D&E. And I think that's fine. Just like there's lots of doctors that don't do other surgeries that they're not trained to do."

However, lack of training opportunities accounts for only part of the resistance to change. Labor induction is an emotionally and physically easier process for *physicians*. They administer medications and then leave the patient to labor overnight in the hospital with nursing staff—often on the hospital labor and delivery ward in earshot of crying newborns. Nurses must support the woman, sometimes while simultaneously caring for women giving birth to full-term live babies, and the patient can be left to deal with delivering the dead fetus alone or with a nurse (Kaltreider, Goldsmith, and Margolis 1979). Physicians see the patient after the delivery, often performing a surgical procedure to scrape the uterine wall to make sure all uterine contents are removed (blood clots, placenta). An induction of labor can take about twenty-four hours. The medications given are strong and can cause intense nausea, vomiting, and diarrhea. In fact, physician and abortion researcher David Grimes (2008) argues that the very reason inductions are so unpleasant is because the second trimester is an evolutionarily disadvantageous time for the body to go into labor. This logic holds that the body is inclined to get rid of unhealthy fetuses early or to hold on until they are ready for birth. The argument he makes is supported by the fact that hormonally inducing the uterus to contract and abort a pregnancy in the second trimester takes much higher doses of medication than in the beginning of pregnancy (for miscarriage completion or abortion) or the end (to induce a full-term birth), making for an extremely uncomfortable experience for the second-trimester patient.

The shift in recent years from labor induction to D&Es means a shift of the burden of the difficult procedure from the patient and nurse to the physician (Kaltreider, Goldsmith, and Margolis 1979; Lohr 2008). A D&E requires less physical effort on the part of the patient and is much shorter in duration (fifteen to thirty minutes). One or two days before the abortion, patients usually have seaweed dilators (laminaria) inserted into the cervix, an uncomfortable but quick office procedure. From that point, while the woman is at home (or in some cases a hotel), the dilators slowly expand the opening into the uterus, making the procedure safer, technically easier, and less painful than it would be otherwise. However, the next step, removing a second-trimester fetus with surgical instruments, can be a visually disturbing and physically strenuous procedure for the physician. Therefore, D&Es are widely believed to be easier on patients but harder on doctors.

Little by little, training programs have transitioned to D&Es for second-trimester abortion, but some programs have dragged their feet in making that change (Eastwood et al. 2006). In the southern region surrounding the one residency program I studied without D&E training, I found that induction of labor was still the preferred method of a seemingly high number of private-practice physicians. These doctors told me they sent their private-practice patients to maternal–fetal medicine doctors (perinatologists) for induction of labor, except in the following case of Dr. Kelly Paz in the large southern city of the residency:

> In this practice there's one doctor here who's sixty-seven years old. And he does up to twenty-two-week D&Es. He is amazing, but he's sixty-seven and he's going to retire. And I don't have that much experience with the higher [gestations]. And everybody in this area sends all of their [miscarriages of] sixteen to twenty-two weeks to him, or anomalies to him. And one of these days he's going to retire and there's going to be a void.
>
> There was actually a situation a couple of years ago where we had an eighteen-week [miscarriage]. They [tried to induce labor with drugs] for two days . . . and nothing happened, and they had called for this doctor, and this doctor was out of town. And it actually ended up being a very bad outcome because the patient went into DIC . . . [11]
>
> We appreciate him because Lord, let me tell you, he saves our butt. So the fact that on his time off he works at [these abortion] clinics—is a blessing to us because we always know we have a good person to send our patients to.

In reality, the private-practice physicians I interviewed in the South are probably unaware of the elective abortions that their patients undergo, which lends a skewed image to the prevalence of labor induction. Physicians speculated that patients do not necessarily tell them about unintended pregnancies and abortions out of embarrassment, usually going directly to an abortion clinic for care. Abortion referrals made to maternal–fetal medicine physicians were largely for genetic anomalies, which were generally perceived as more medically legitimate abortions. Thus, even though an ob-gyn would have enough training to perform a labor induction, these procedures are sent to subspecialists, which additionally legitimates and medicalizes the abortion.

There is another important dimension to why induction is still practiced in the United States aside from lack of skilled providers and specific cultures of practice that are slow to change. Some psychological studies have shown that in cases of pregnancy loss or anomaly, the ability to see and hold the intact fetus allows patients a healthier grieving process and better recovery (Kirk 1984). Also, in some cases an autopsy can be important for helping to determine the cause of fetal anomaly or death. Again, this is possible only if the fetus is intact. A few physicians are skilled at the surgical removal of an intact fetus, but this is the very type of procedure targeted by the ban on so-called partial-birth abortion.

While induction is widely hailed to be psychological beneficial for certain patients for these reasons, there is some lack of consensus on the issue (Hughes and Riches 2003). Dr. Thompson shared her own strong opinions to the contrary in the context of telling me about her personal experience with pregnancy loss. She miscarried at twenty-two weeks of pregnancy. It happened so rapidly that she was unable to choose a method of intervention; she delivered spontaneously. But when I asked her what she would have done if she had had to decide between D&E and induction, she responded: "I would have a D&E . . . It is too difficult, I think, to have a delivery, personally. But that's me and everybody's different. But you know, all the geneticists when they talk about, 'Oh, if we just had that autopsy!' I never once had a patient where that made a difference."

Furthermore, one study of patients terminating pregnancies for fetal anomalies showed the same level of satisfaction among women who chose D&E and women who chose induction (Burgoine et al. 2005). The researchers concluded, as others studying medical versus surgical abortion in the first trimester had done before (Jensen, Harvey, and Beckman 2000), that perhaps the most important factor in patient satisfaction is the patient's ability to select the option that she wants. This small degree of personal freedom in a difficult situation, they believe, contributes to women's satisfaction with the method chosen. While this finding may not be surprising, it settles some debates about how to determine which method is best for the patient and points to the psychological benefit of having choices.

The Personal Is Political

When Dr. Anderson and I were discussing her experiences providing abortion in private practice after residency, I asked her how her patients choose between labor induction and D&E if they decide to terminate a pregnancy for fetal anomalies (since these are the only terminations allowed in her practice). She explained:

> You know, I think it's a really difficult decision for them. It's interesting. I think some of the people do it based on, "I need to get this done and get it over with and not think about it." And so they will choose the D&E and kind of move on. I think there are people who are scared about a surgical procedure and so I think that plays a role as well. So they kind of lean more towards the induction.
>
> I actually end up taking care of a lot of the patients because I'm one of the few that can do D&Es . . . Although I feel like most people end up choosing induction anyway . . . [I] might be a little biased in my counseling because we have a wonderful perinatal loss program at our hospital. And so when they go through the induction process, then they go through that whole—you know, [they] get pictures [of the baby] and [have] all the supports and things that for a lot of people is good for healing. [With D&Es] I will still give them some books about loss and stuff . . . [but] you can't take pictures, you can't have them see the baby afterwards.

This is when Dr. Anderson shifted from her role as physician to her experience as a patient. It turned out that she had been faced with making that same decision herself after she found out in the second trimester of her pregnancy that her baby had a fatal diagnosis. Regarding her own loss, she explained that she ended up making a choice that surprised even her:

> Actually, with our daughter we were faced with the same decision. And in the end we actually ended up choosing perinatal hospice.[12] Kind of funny, how life takes you. We got all of her diagnoses and so I—we have the Women's Right-to-Know Act in [here] where you have to sign the forms twenty-four hours in advance [of getting an abortion]—you read all the stuff verbatim[13] . . . And I called my [practice] partner and my friend and I'm like, "Okay, I'm coming to the hospital tomorrow. I'm signing the forms. We'll induce over the weekend."
>
> And then I changed my mind. You know, for me there was no—I don't really know, you know, it was kind of the inner voice that said, "Don't do it. Maybe you might get time with her or something." And we ultimately, we did, we got ten days with her.

Dr. Anderson decided to try to carry her nonviable pregnancy to term. She had a strong feeling, not one that she was able to articulate in detail, that she wanted to know her baby even if the baby would be dead upon delivery or die soon after birth. At the time that she received the fatal diagnoses, she had more than four months left of pregnancy. "We just waited to see whatever would happen," she said. "And I actually thought she was probably going to die in utero but she didn't . . . And then we ended up going into labor and having a regular labor up here [in the hospital] . . . They had said with one of the birth defects that she had, only about 3 percent make it to term, so we felt pretty lucky from that respect." Before Dr. Anderson's interview, I had thought that the continuation of a nonviable pregnancy was a trajectory chosen primarily by religious women who strictly opposed abortion or women who lacked resources to pursue second-trimester abortion. Dr. Anderson is neither of these.

Dr. Anderson continued to work and interact with colleagues, patients, family members, and friends to whom she openly disclosed the fatal nature of her fetus' anomalies. She was self-conscious about appearing that she was continuing the pregnancy for religious or political reasons. "I do think there are people who probably think, 'Oh, she must be very pro-life,' because of the choice that we made," she said. "And you know, I keep my views to myself, for the most part . . . Nobody said that, but I've had patients and other providers kind of hint at that." But Dr. Anderson maintains that "people can be pro-choice and still choose other options," as she did. She did not want to become political around her personal decision, yet she noticed how abortion politics surfaced during the course of her pregnancy whether she liked it or not:

> There are some websites and some local groups that support women who have adverse pregnancy diagnoses or special needs. And I communicated with some of them, despite the fact that I could tell they were very pro-life. I could always kind of pick and choose that way, look past it. But there was this one that I had been communicating with, and I noticed on their website, when I went back and looked at it later, that they have a link to "Pro-Life OB/GYNs," whatever that organization is, the American Association of Pro-Life OB/GYNs or something. And I thought "Oh, no, don't, I hope they don't add me into that link."

While she did not believe she had actually been added to the site, she stated in passing that she suspected that certain colleagues had referred patients to her who were seeking an ob-gyn who opposed abortion since she made the decision not to abort.

When I asked Dr. Anderson whether her personal experience with the loss of her baby had changed any of her feelings about providing abortion, she explained that her support for abortion rights has remained the same, but she is more sensitive about the issue in ways that she was still, at the time of the interview, trying to understand. For example, she pondered whether she would counsel patients any differently about how to manage fetal anomalies:

> I haven't counseled any patients since I've been in that situation, but I have taken care of them since I've been in that situation. But I don't think I would use that as influencing people in delivery versus D&E. But I think it's a hard decision because what you may feel one moment could change the next day. And sometimes I think people just make the decision kind of quickly and then may not have time to really think about all the implications of it. Because you're so stunned when you first get that news.

Thus, she does not think she would give biased advice to patients, pushing them to carry their nonviable fetuses to term and go through perinatal hospice, as she did, instead of terminating the pregnancy. However, her experience has made her concerned that patients allow themselves time to understand the psychological implications of the different paths. In terms of her future in elective abortion care, she still believes someday—perhaps after retirement—she may moonlight at Planned Parenthood like some of her colleagues. But she became aware that she feels slightly more critical of certain women's abortion decisions than she used to: "You get into the judgmental thing, you know. The 'someone-who's-had-seven-abortions-versus-a-person-who's-having-one' kind of thing. So I think there are situations like that where I have probably a little bit [of the feeling that] it's not fair. There are always people who are trying to have babies. And so, I mean, it changed my perspective a little but hasn't—not completely."

Thus, her experience somewhat diminished her ability to empathize with abortion patients. I heard similar realizations from a handful of physicians who, after having children, battling infertility, or treating infertile patients, noticed new judgments arising about women with unwanted pregnancies that surprised their pro-choice sensibilities. Dr. Anderson elaborated by explaining that despite some changes in her personal feelings, she holds in high regard the value of patient autonomy and choice free from physician ideology:

> I would never want to be a doctor that just goes, "This is the way that it's supposed to be done" and [not be] open to other options or discussions based on what's best for the patient. . . . the whole patriarchal type—telling a patient this is what you need to do and not giving them a say in it, an option or discussion—I would never want to be that way. I see that. And I think some of that is gender and some of that's an age-related thing where doctors used to just tell patients, "This is what you need to do," and those are your only options. But that's not the way medicine is anymore.

Thus, invoking the ethics of personal freedom, Dr. Anderson maintains that she wants her patients to be able to make the choices that are right for them.

Summary

Dr. Anderson's experience as a physician and a patient exposed many layers of decision making around abortion. Her story unlinks politics from practice in poignant ways. While a medical student, she was enmeshed in an antiabortion network of friends; but through exposure to abortion practice during residency, she changed her mind about providing abortions. After graduating residency, she performed abortions on patients with fetal anomalies regularly, but when she had her own fetal anomaly, she chose not to have an abortion. And while she waited for her pregnancy to come to a natural and unfortunate end, she chose not to embed herself in the antiabortion universe that supported her emotionally, but rather to continue navigating a middle path of her own creation.

Many physicians, like Dr. Anderson, resist a black-and-white morality around abortion and fetal life. More consistent among abortion providers is the belief that fetal life is what it means to the woman carrying the fetus—that pregnant women determine the meaning for themselves. Physicians often take up that meaning when they attempt to understand patients' reasons for seeking abortion, and sometimes they impose their own as well. Some such impositions at times become visible in the methods physicians use in abortion care—what they regard as best for patients and best for themselves. Some abortion patients are sent to specialists and given psychological support, and others are sent to high-volume abortion clinics, and still others are sent to the phone book. Dr. Anderson exemplified respect for individual choice both in the way she was attentive to her own "inner voice" and in how she continually asserted the need to listen to the particular preferences of women who may want or need to terminate a pregnancy.

CHAPTER 5

Practice Constraints and the Institutionalized Buck-Passing of Abortion Care

I had a lot [of residents] that were just 100 percent pro-choice who have never done an abortion in private practice . . . In a conservative state like [this one in the Midwest], if you get the reputation that your group performs abortions, all of a sudden the other groups have a marked increase in their patient load.

DR. DAVIS CHASEY, *retired founder and director of a residency abortion clinic*

For decades, abortion rights activists and scholars have argued that abortion should be integrated into mainstream medical care and hence treated as a legitimate part of full-spectrum reproductive health services (Lindheim 1979; Rose 2007). In theory, getting abortion services out of the clinics and into doctors' offices would reduce stigma and make abortion care less marginalized and vulnerable to violent attack by antiabortionists. To many in the pro-choice movement, this seems a straightforward solution requiring only the politicization of physicians and their commitment to continuing to provide abortions after residency. However, this strategy fails to take into account the substantial decline in physician autonomy since the dominance of managed care. Although numerous physicians have become politically active around abortion during medical school and residency,[1] the commitment appears to be too costly for most physicians to sustain. The *willing* physicians in this chapter explain how integrating abortion into mainstream medical services is quite difficult. Mainstream medicine passed the buck on abortion long ago, and many physicians find it both regrettable and easier that way.

Abortion Stigma, Professional Civility, and Conservative Community Pressure

In many parts of the country, both urban and rural, the legacy of the pre-*Roe* "abortionist" is alive and well. The stigma associated with this label is pervasive yet unusual as far as stigmas go in that this one is associated with an otherwise high-status individual: a physician. Regardless, the label is "deeply discrediting," in the words of Erving Goffman, from his seminal introduction of stigma to the field of sociology (Goffman 1963: 3). The word *abortionist* confers the imagery of a physician who does little else besides abortion and may be not skillful enough to do well in general or mainstream medicine. It also connotes bad intentions. In Carole Joffe's study of doctors who provided abortion before legalization, one physician remembered that " 'abortionist' was such a dirty word, it was just one step above pervert, or child abuser . . . to be called an abortionist in the 1950s, you were the scum of the earth" (Joffe 1995: 76). Also, by the mere association with abortion, especially at that time, doctors were seen as condoning a "sexually immoral" lifestyle. Remarking on how perceptions of physicians providing illegal abortions (and those parading as physicians) affected future generations of abortion providers, Joffe writes, "Abortion practices in the pre-*Roe* period created a complex legacy for physicians active after *Roe*, given the enduring images of inept 'quacks' and 'butchers' and the associations with criminality and greed" (Joffe 1995: 52). After legalization, some of Joffe's abortion providers found that their status increased little and that the label abortionist stuck in certain medical environments, regardless of the legal legitimization. One physician objected, "I'm no more an abortionist than I am an obstetrician or a hysterectomist or any other procedure that I do" (Joffe 1995: 153).

In a review of the sociological literature on stigma since Goffman (1963), Bruce Link and Jo Phelan (2001) found four principles consistent among stigmas. These can be applied neatly to abortion providers. First, Link and Phelan argue that stigmas are widely used to distinguish and label difference—as in *abortionist* rather than *ob-gyn* or *physician*. Second, the label is associated with a negative attribute, in this case, a morally deficient or technically incompetent physician. Third, the stigma allows the user to separate "us" from "them," much as the "quack" is singled out from legitimate physicians. Finally, status loss and discrimination result— exactly what was feared by several physicians in my study and widely experienced decades ago by Joffe's abortion-providing physicians.

Many physicians I spoke with, like Joffe's physician, regard the idea of being labeled for one of the many surgical procedures they perform as absurd. For those in small-town private practices, however, the prospect of being identified with abortion in this way is profoundly threatening. For example, Dr. Bill Spellman in the Midwest said: "I didn't plan on doing abortions in my private practice for a lot of reasons. It's too small of a community to really do *that* . . . it's tough if you do abortions electively in your own private practice because then you get labeled as an *abortionist*, which, a guy [here], he got labeled like that." Similarly, regarding his small southern town, Dr. Kevin Dougherty remarked, "There's a history in the city that I'm in. There was a practice that did offer abortions and were *run out of town*."

The subjects at the center of this controversy, physicians, are normally high-status individuals; they have a long way to fall from grace. Additionally, the individuals in my study were often new parents, new homeowners, new members of a practice—all, of course, because I selected a group that had graduated only five to ten years before from their residency programs. Therefore, many saw themselves as relatively vulnerable—an unlikely characterization of physicians. These doctors had student loans and mortgages to repay; at the same time, they needed to prove themselves as worthy members of their private-practice groups.

Dr. John Brill wanted to continue providing abortions in his private practice, as he had done in his first job after residency, but after moving to a small, conservative town in the West to be closer to family, he no longer saw it as a possibility. "It's a small town and none of the ob-gyns perform abortions," he said. "There is one abortion clinic in town. And the provider who comes up from [the city two and a half hours away] to perform abortions is *vilified* within the community. To perform abortions in this community means being '*evil*.'"

For Dr. Brill, it was as if he had entered a new world. He recently had come from a western urban area where he was, among other things, an abortion provider. Yet his move placed him in a cultural and political context where he quickly decided he must hide that identity. With the aforementioned commuting provider planning to retire soon, Dr. Brill was contacted by the local abortion clinic in its search for a new physician director: "They called me up and said, 'Hey, we heard that you might be the person.' I was like, 'Well, you know, that's real nice but I don't think I can be the guy running the [abortion] clinic.'. . . I didn't turn them down. I said I'd be happy to have a dialogue, but I don't think I can be, you know, 'Doctor Abortion Provider,' the only one in this town." This was not a simple decision for Dr. Brill. Politically, he is very sympathetic to abortion rights; however, he is deeply concerned that any connection to abortion would undermine him professionally:

> It's frustrating because it's a service that is desperately needed, and it would completely destroy my ability to practice medicine in town. And that's a difficult position to be in. Do I sacrifice myself for the greater good? But then I can't take care of my wife and kids? I don't like thinking about it too much. It sort of burns me when I have to think about it too much . . . It's a real sort of strong Christian community, so a lot of the family practice docs in town, they're strong Christians. And that's your referral base. And so to be labeled as the evil abortion doctor is a great way to make no friends amongst the ob-gyns and to have no family practice docs refer patients to you.

Dr. Brill identified professional failure, and the economic effect of that on his family, as a major risk to providing abortions. He worried that other physicians would not refer their patients to him and his practice would be, in a sense, boycotted by the community. For Dr. Brill and doctors similarly situated, the local stigma of abortion is both palpable and personal.

Some physicians had the unpleasant experience of being screened by patients with strong antiabortion views, further reiterating the sentiment that abortion practice is risky for their reputations in their communities and the financial success of the medical groups with which they practice. Five of the six doctors who shared these stories practice in the Midwest in cities of varying sizes. One such physician, Dr. Stacy Kern, had an uncomfortable encounter with a couple who were looking for a physician who, like themselves, would be opposed to abortion:

> I had a patient who came in for obstetrical care with me as a new ob patient . . . And we had about a forty-minute new [prenatal] visit, which is a long time, because we had a lot of stuff to talk about. And at the very end of the discussion her husband said to me, "Well, we just feel so much more comfortable with you because we've had some experiences where practitioners think it's okay to, like, do abortions or something. And I just don't see how anybody could ever believe that—you know, to deliver babies and then to kill babies and to be okay with that" . . .
>
> Well, first I thought, oh dear . . . And I just sort of looked [at them] and I said, "Well, you're talking to one of those people" . . . Oh my God, the room was just like—there's this deep inhalation . . . I said, "Listen, I'm sorry but, you know, if somebody needs a safe procedure, I feel that you have to offer them a safe procedure . . . I'll step out and you two can talk and I'll be back in a few minutes." And I stepped out and actually had a family practice resident shadowing me that day. When we got through, her eyes were [bulging wide]. And I said, "I don't think she'll be staying with me" . . . Well, about five minutes later I went back, and they're all packed up [and said,] "We'll be going elsewhere."

While disconcerting to Dr. Kern, the interaction ended peacefully. Dr. Bill Spellman was not so lucky, and in his case, the patient was initially deceptive, which eroded his confidence in counseling patients about pregnancy options for the future:

> I got burnt on it once so I'm always leery. A woman came in and started talking to me directly about how she wanted to get a termination. She brought it up, she wanted to talk about it, and so I said, "Well, there's this and this and this available out there." And she says, "Would there be any way that you could perform this? I really think that we have a link here and I really want you to do this." And I felt very bad for her because of the whole story behind it. And I said, "Well," I said, "I've done these before." And right then she stood up and she said, "I knew it. I knew it all along. You're a baby killer," and walked out of the room . . . She wrote this long letter to the people who ran the office that I worked for basically telling them just what an absolute scumbag I was and all these other

things. So since that point—you know, burned once, I'm not going to do it again—when somebody comes in and wants to talk about [abortion], I talk to them a little bit, I have them leave, and I have them come back for another visit.

Dr. Spellman now gives patients with unwanted pregnancies reading materials about pregnancy options from ACOG, a presumably uncontroversial source of information, and talks to them at the second visit about whether they want a referral to an abortion clinic. He feels this has successfully weeded out one or two similar patients, but he credits the professional embarrassment and personal discomfort of this interaction with making him even more sensitive to the stigma and contention surrounding abortion in his community.

Physicians practicing in small and midsized towns worried significantly about the consequences of involvement with abortion. Most of these doctors practiced in groups where policies on abortion are made for the practice as a whole. Dr. Spellman thinks it would be challenging to persuade the partners of his midwestern group practice to provide abortions in their town even if they did want to:

> If you start doing elective terminations in your practice, then the community will just kind of view you as that one thing. The right-to-life people are really, really, really organized in this and they're very, very good about getting that word out within seconds about somebody. And, you know, it's—you hate to say it—you practice in the real world . . . I think if we were in LA or in Phoenix, Arizona, or something like that, I don't think the partners would give a crap. Because it's such a big place that, you know, who cares if two or three thousand or a hundred thousand people believe that you're an abortion clinic when there's still 2.4 million more people out there? Here we only have a couple hundred thousand people . . . They guard their reputation a lot in these communities. It's one of the things that really makes a practice.

Essentially, he argues that performing abortions means facing professional sanctions such as losing patients and losing business, that the anti-abortion activists will bring so much attention to the matter that the entire ob-gyn practice will be viewed as "an abortion clinic." Whether practicing solo or in a group, doctors in relatively small or politically conservative communities felt a stigma that made abortion practice seem incompatible with general medical practice.

Most of the physicians in my study feared the social and professional consequences of performing abortions and maintained collegiality and civility by not performing them after residency. Those I spoke with who performed abortions regularly, and not exclusively for genetic or medical indications, lived in areas around the country that were less politically conservative and/or worked in relatively protective university settings where multiple layers of bureaucracy as well as the way that the clinic is physically embedded within a larger medical facility made them less visible to the outside world. Indeed, almost all of the physicians I interviewed trained in such protective university environments. Graduation was a rude awakening for some.

Threats, Intimidation, and Violence

Not all professional sanctions were feared, anticipated, and then avoided. Some physicians reported having direct confrontations with colleagues regarding abortion. An important characteristic of most stigmas is that their subjects must agree to the "rules"; that is, they must recognize that they are stigmatized, and if they do not, there will be consequences for such "deviance" (Goffman 1963).[2] Those with power over the stigmatized may impose the consequences in the form of direct discrimination (Link and Phelan 2001). Physicians encounter various types of intimidation and violence when they provide (or consider providing) abortions. These can be viewed as a type of such stigma enforcement. Several physicians I spoke with who wanted to continue performing abortions met with uncomfortable interactions out in the "real world." Indeed, these interactions were uncomfortable enough to keep them "in line" and to significantly shape their practice patterns.

Many physicians found out at job interviews how abortion would be viewed in the private practices they hoped to join. Some declined job offers because of abortion prohibitions, and some did not. Still others had little choice in the matter given the limited job opportunities in their area. For example, Dr. Kern was tied to the area because of her husband's work.

She took a job in one of the two existing ob-gyn practices in her midsized city in the Midwest, and by the time I met her she had worked in both. Speaking of the second group practice, she said: "In this group, you interview with all of the different physicians that are partners. And the one partner who's very senior in the group and very pro-life, basically his only job is to sit with you and just tell you . . . 'If you join this group you will not be performing abortion procedures. And if that's a problem for you, then you will work elsewhere. Okay?'"

Dr. Kern's experience of being told by her superior that abortion would not be tolerated in his practice was not unique. Dr. Kevin Dougherty's first job was in a small town in the South. He was unsure of his personal intent to provide abortions, but the group let him know quickly that it was not an option. He was not surprised by this, however. He explained to me why he felt it was important to respect a medical group's desire to avoid abortion:

> My feeling about it is that everybody is pinned down by their business climate—I mean, my business climate right now is absolutely antagonistic towards even the idea of *this* . . . In private practice, you certainly don't want—if you get a sense that *that* is not going to go over well, you don't push *that* . . . it's not just your own practice [that] is in jeopardy, but you're also putting your partners' practice in jeopardy by being associated with them . . . They knew that I had done *that* in the past. They made clear undertones about the fact that, "You know, we're not going to be doing *that*."—"Okay, got it!" And I don't feel strongly enough about it to, to say, "I'm going to do it and go out and"—You know, there's only so much up-starting that you can do, especially without having a lot of your own patients yet. So I have remained fairly quiescent about it.

Dr. Dougherty did not want to "make waves" so early in his career. In addition to maintaining professional civility with his private-practice partners, he worried, as Dr. Brill did, about having enough patients and losing business by being associated with abortion. Because medicine has remained largely privatized in the United States, physician practices are subject to market forces like all other businesses.

Dr. Spellman, like Dr. Kern, had limited job choices because he wanted to stay close to family. He took a job in a private practice in a midwestern urban area where he was told point-blank not to do abortions and was even threatened:

> The guy that I replaced out there . . . I don't know how old he was. He looked ancient to me when I first met him. And I took over his patient practice. So they'd already interviewed me and accepted me for the job and I already signed the contract. So I went out there and—I don't even know why I was riding around with this guy—but he took me to lunch and . . . we get back to his office and I was supposed to follow him in on a few patients for—I don't even know the real reasons. But he leaned across the desk and said, *"If I ever find out you did elective abortion any time in your professional life, you'll never practice medicine in [this state] again. Do you understand that?"* And I went, "Okay." And he goes, "As far as I know, you've never done an abortion, have you?" And I said, "Yeah, a lot for genetic reasons and lots of other things." He said, "From this point on out—I'll take that as you saying no—from this point on." And I'm thinking to myself, you're leaving this practice. You have nothing to do with it. You don't even own it. So it kind of rankled me a little bit that he came across that strong.

This was a very disturbing way for Dr. Spellman to start his career. However, as he suspected, the older physician had less power to manage his future practice than he threatened during that conversation:

> I thought, "Yep, that just confirms it. I just can't do abortion electively in clinic." But I said to my partners, "But there's a need for people that have (A) genetic problems, and (B) have, you know, [fetal] demises. And if you don't have somebody to do these [abortions], what are they going to do? [Are] you going to do hysterectomies on these people?" . . . And they're like, "Well, we'll figure out a way." So one thing led to another, and boom, boom, boom, I got referrals, usually one or two a week, of [abortions] to do over that time of people with either [fetal] demises or with severe genetic anomalies or other anomalies.

Such a turn of the tides is not an uncommon abortion story. Many physicians want both distance from abortion and someone skilled to send their patients to; this is part of what Joffe considers to be the deep ambivalence around abortion in American medicine (Joffe 1995). While many physician organizations publicly take an antiabortion stance, individual physicians often empathize with the predicaments of their patients, especially when they involve fetal anomalies. Dr. Spellman's colleagues had to refer their patients to him because they had not been trained or had not maintained their surgical skills in second-trimester abortions and could not perform these procedures safely even if they had wanted to. His partners were grateful that they had a conveniently located physician to, in a certain sense, do their "dirty work," a term used sociologically by Everett Hughes to describe work that is perceived as unsavory and/or degrading, but necessary (Hughes and Coser 1994). That is, although Dr. Spellman's partners may have been unwilling or unable to participate in abortion training and care, on some level they understood certain abortions as necessary for their patients. The relatively tolerant practice culture was short-lived, however. Dr. Spellman continued:

> And then as time went on, another partner came to the group who was super conservative as far as his thoughts about most issues in the world. And he wanted me to sign a contract with the group that said I would not do terminations on certain genetic problems like [Down syndrome] and things like that, because they weren't fatal anomalies . . . he was just him being him trying to control things, which is what he did with all aspects of the practice, not just that. I would never sign anything like that as long as I live.

Dr. Spellman resisted control by both his predecessor and his colleague, to an extent. But as he mentioned, he quickly gave up any expectation of doing elective abortions because of the strength of the stigma and the antiabortion sentiment in his region.

Midwesterners and small-town physicians were not the only ones to feel personally threatened by the stigma and controversy of abortion in their practices. Dr. Qui Qan Wong took a job in what she described as a highly Catholic northeastern suburb near her residency after graduation. She was surprised how her medical practices were policed by staff members at the hospital, which she described as a public and not religiously affiliated institution. She first learned that abortion would not be acceptable in her practice when she tried to schedule a second-trimester abortion for a fatal genetic indication. Dr. Wong explained that since she did not grow up assimilated into American culture, she was quite surprised to discover that abortion was such a polarizing issue:

> You know, maybe it's my stupidity. I didn't realize there was that much, you know, antiabortion feeling out there. I guess in residency, you just live [in the hospital], so you don't get as much outside. It wasn't until I started to be on my own, I started to feel this sort of real antiabortion environment that we have . . .
>
> One [case] that really wasn't an abortion but it was for medical reasons . . . and I felt that it should be done, you know, because I had a relationship with the patient, [but I] was told, "No way"—and had the nurses come and say, "You are not doing that" . . . . It was a fetal anomaly . . . that baby wasn't going to survive no matter what. And even that, they won't let me do it . . . I called . . . and [the surgery scheduler] said, "Wait a minute," and then they got somebody else on the phone with me and said, "You can't do it."

An abortion for a fetal anomaly, especially a fatal one, was not considered a "moral" issue in Dr. Wong's residency program. As her words convey, it was considered medically necessary. But she soon learned that no abortion was considered necessary in her new hospital culture, and although she had preferred to take care of her patient herself, she ultimately referred the patient to her residency abortion service.

Dr. Wong was shocked to discover that even pharmacists were involved in her practices around abortion,[3] through a very threatening conflict over a drug that is associated with medication abortion but widely used for other conditions as well:

> I have pharmacists who call me who refuse to give the medication Cytotec.[4] They said, "That's abortion medication, I'm not going to give it," even though the time that he called me about wasn't for abortion. It was for a [different gynecological] issue. He said, "I know that's abortion," and I was like, "Well, that's not what I'm using it for," and he said, "I'm not going to give it." And he started yelling at me on the phone and said, "I'm going to put your name on the Web!"
>
> He was threatening me . . . He said, "Well, I refuse and I'm tearing up the prescription so she's not going to get it anywhere else." So the poor lady had to come back and get the prescription . . . I was just like, my

God! But there are a few of them around [this northeastern urban area]—pharmacists—who, literally, will not fill Cytotec.

By threatening Dr. Wong with posting her name on the Web, the pharmacist threatened to publicly name her as an abortion provider to potentially violent antiabortion activists. This was not a threat she took lightly. An abortion provider had been shot at the local abortion clinic only a few years before.

Fear of violence was not nearly as prevalent in the physician interviews as I would have thought, but it was noticeably more salient for those who had practiced near protesters or near victims of violence. Dr. Tiffany Howell had significant exposure to protesters when she moonlighted for an abortion clinic in a western urban area. By the time of the interview, she had moved to a conservative midsized city in the Midwest.

> The antiabortion forces are definitely real and they're definitely out there and can make your life hard. In [the city were I worked before,] they picketed [the abortion clinic] every day, and the doctors that had been working there for years and years and years had people at their house all the time, picketing at their house—one of them had sent flyers to all his neighbors talking about how he was an abortionist and all this kind of—so they make it difficult for you . . .
>
> I didn't go [work at the clinic] as often [as the other doctors]—but [the protesters] eventually figured out who I was and they found out what my name was . . . they would yell your name out as you're walking into the clinic and stuff and take your picture. And it's intimidating. It's intimidating as a provider. And when you go to [work there], they ask you if you want to have a bulletproof vest to wear and you're like, "Oh, dear". . . . But it's true, people have been shot who are abortion providers. It has happened . . . I'd like to do abortions, but I don't know if I'll ever do them here.

In recent decades, the label abortionist has done more than signify stigma and defamation that could result in professional failure. It has been used to identify targets of violence. And those who have not accepted the terms of the stigma (that they should not provide abortions, and if they do it should be hidden) have at times experienced violence in the form of clinic or physician attack. Stigma and violence as well as economic and professional failure are what physicians fear. These are the perceived and real risks of involvement with abortion care and the reasons why many individuals, group practices, and large institutions distance themselves from abortion practice.

No-Abortion Policies

Physicians in all areas of the country referred to *no-abortion policies* in their private-practice groups, HMOs, and hospitals, although they rarely used those words. Unlike their approach to any other medical procedure, and for reasons unrelated to skill level or technological resources, many medical groups make a concerted effort to take a stand on whether they provide abortions or not. Sometimes the reasoning for this appeared individual and arbitrary, as in the cases above where a superior had anti-abortion sentiments and was able to control the practice of employed physicians. But the widespread existence of these prohibitions betrays their structural nature as a response to the stigma and contention surrounding abortion and results in the institutionalized buck-passing of abortion care.

Only one physician I spoke with, Dr. Brill, is in private practice alone. Consistent with the major shifts in medicine toward managed care during the past few decades (Freidson 1970; Hafferty and Light 1995; Hartley 2002; Haug 1988; Madison and Konrad 1988), the rest of the physicians practice in large private-practice groups, HMOs, the military, or academic institutions. Physician autonomy over decisions about abortion practice is severely curtailed by this restructuring. Physicians found out both informally and formally about the abortion policies in their practice settings. Abortion "policies" were conveyed in a variety of ways beyond threats and intimidation. Such policies were observed in order to avoid conflict. The protocols determining how abortions get done and who does them differed widely, but the tendency to separate them from other aspects of ob-gyn care, and for coworkers to police those boundaries, was similar in cities around the country, both big and small.

Some physicians learned at a job interview, in a nonthreatening way, what the abortion policy of a practice would be; however, the effect was the same as in the cases in which physicians learned more pointedly that abortion was not acceptable in a practice. For example, Dr. Janie Cheng, practicing in a midsized city in the Midwest, remembered: "When I joined this group, at first they did bring up that during my interviews to say, 'Is it okay that we do not perform abortion? Do you have any religious or, you know, personal belief against that?' I say, 'No, it's not a problem.' So they say, 'It's a historical reason that we feel that society will look at us differently if we perform abortions' . . . So they decided not to perform abortions as an ob-gyn group."

Similar to Dr. Cheng, Dr. Janine Graham knew going into her first job after residency that her private practice in a midwestern urban area did not allow elective abortions. In fact, because of her extensive second-trimester abortion training, she was asked to be on her medical group's abortion committee that reviews which genetic and medically indicated abortions are acceptable to the practice.

> The policy that we have is basically no elective abortions. We have an abortion committee, which I happen to be on, that reviews medically indicated abortions and inductions . . . Typically, it's either a fetal anomaly that perinatology has stated there's basically no chance of life, or if there are extreme medical indications for the mother. If the pregnancy would put her [health] at risk, it's a gray zone. The committee is made up of different specialties—family practice, pediatrics, a chaplain. And so whenever a case comes up, we discuss it and then most of the time we approve it . . . If they're not considered a medical risk or if they're not fatal, then we do refer those out . . .
>
> I asked one of my senior partners who's been at the clinic a long time about the no-abortion policy, and [that person] said that that just goes . . . back historically, I think obviously before *Roe v. Wade*, and then when that happened there were people on the board at that time who made that decision, and I guess it's just never really been challenged.

Not all practices are as explicit, and some physicians find out indirectly how their practices deal with abortion after they start working. Unlike Drs. Cheng and Graham, Dr. Stephanie Fulton, working in an urban area in the South, was not told up front about her private practice group's abortion policy. "It didn't come up at all in interviewing," she said. "Like I said, it wasn't a question I really asked. I guess I just found it out as I started . . . Essentially, we have our referral book, and that's how it came up." She learned from a colleague that elective abortions were referred to abortion clinics, and genetic or medical terminations were referred to a group of maternal–fetal medicine physicians, a common separation that has more social than medical significance.[5]

Abortions can be performed in doctors' offices, unless the patient is in the second trimester or has certain health problems, but many physicians do not like to do surgical procedures in their offices, or their practice prohibits it. Therefore, physicians usually schedule surgery at a nearby hospital or ambulatory surgery center. But these places often have their own policies regarding abortion, which may or may not be explicit. Dr. Anne Radik learned from coworkers that her nonsectarian hospital in a large western metropolitan area did not allow abortions, largely because of staff resistance.

> I have no problem doing them, but the hospital here doesn't like it when we do them . . . it's a public hospital . . . I don't know if the nurses don't want to be part of it or they all just like to band together and say they don't want to be part of it. Because if you're the one that says you don't mind doing it, everyone else is going to look at you. So if there's an abortion procedure that needs to be done, I send them to Planned Parenthood. It's not worth my time and effort to jump through the hoops of the hospital to make that happen for an elective termination . . . I've only been in practice for two years, and actually in my first couple months in practice— the people that are in my office here told me, "Don't even bother."

Dr. Radik was not particularly interested in doing abortions, so she was quickly deterred by her office mates' advice not to struggle with the staff resistance at the hospital. However, it is easy to see in this example how abortion practice patterns are shaped by hearsay and warnings that maintain a particular medical culture of practice.

Dr. Kelly Paz deduced that most abortions were not acceptable at her private nonsectarian hospital in a southern urban area while jumping through hoops to do abortions for patients with fetal anomalies who, by definition, are aborting in the second trimester.[6] "For [the] second trimester," she said, "we have to get five or six signatures for necessity . . . to do it at the hospital . . . Let's say we have a sixteen-week anomaly . . . we have to have a signature from the chief of staff, the maternal–fetal medicine doctor, the ob chief—you have all these signatures that you have to get . . . and that actually made me realize maybe [our hospital] doesn't allow straightforward terminations." Such a rigorous process of signature-procuring harks back to pre-*Roe* days. Before legalization, many hospitals housed abortion committees to decide whether a woman's reason for termination was valid, and signatures of physicians and psychiatrists usually were required.

Some physicians learned which abortion practices would or would not be tolerated through conflicts with colleagues. For example, soon after starting her first job postresidency, Dr. Kern found out that abortions were frowned upon in the practice through a discussion at a meeting of the physicians in her group:

> There came an instant where somebody asked, when RU-486 [mifepristone] first became available [in 2000], if we were going to provide that in the clinic or if we would write prescriptions or if we would be willing to offer that service. And it generated this unbelievable panic in the clinic. And people were very strongly, "No, we are not an abortion clinic. We don't do those kinds of services" . . . And I was just an employee at the time . . . I just kept my mouth shut and didn't say anything.

As a new hire, as opposed to a more powerful practice partner, Dr. Kern did not feel entitled to voice her opinion about abortion. After working at that practice for a couple of years, she decided to go to work for the other ob-gyn group in town, which was much larger and allowed for fewer nights on call per month and, hence, a more family-friendly work schedule. But this group was even less sympathetic to abortion than the first.

Although disappointed, Dr. Kern accepted the fact that she would not provide abortions at either practice, but she was surprised to find out that her practice prohibited her from moonlighting at a small local abortion clinic where she worked during residency. Her practice partners made it very clear that they did not want any legal liability, since the abortion clinic lacked malpractice insurance, nor did they want the stigma of being connected with the clinic through one of their physicians. Dr. Kern took her desire to moonlight to the group, "and they nixed it and said absolutely not. Just because they didn't want my name associated with the clinic."

The abortion clinic had previously relied on the university's malpractice insurance for the residents moonlighting there, but since implementation of the eighty-hour limit on the resident workweek (Fletcher et al. 2005), residents no longer had time to moonlight.[7] Four of the five ob-gyn physicians I interviewed in this state had been approached by the abortion clinic to work as their medical director, and all four of them declined because their own practices would not permit it.

Dr. Kern ran up against the limits of comfort in her group practice when, like Dr. Wong, she tried to schedule a second-trimester abortion for a fatal fetal anomaly which carried the possibility that the pregnant woman herself might develop cancer. The medical consensus for such a pregnancy is that it must be terminated as soon as possible. "I haven't done a D&E here for other anomalies," she said. "It just doesn't happen. I mean, so many people just get routed down to the university, if they want to [terminate] . . . [This patient] wasn't comfortable having to go down there for a procedure, and she didn't know anybody there and it just seemed overwhelming [to her]. She just wanted to stay in the practice that she was comfortable with. And the physician who was taking care of her, himself, didn't perform those procedures, so he asked me."

This occurred around the time when the so-called partial-birth abortion ban was receiving a lot of news attention, and in her confusion about the legalities of the ban, Dr. Kern, while talking with the person at the hospital who schedules her surgeries, wondered aloud whether she could get arrested.

> And I said something about that—it just kind of popped into my head—to the surgery scheduler and somehow it got leaked . . . the clinicians [in our satellite office] heard that I was doing a D&E procedure on a live fetus. And one of the nurses who works over there has a very strong moral feeling about that. She's very pro-life. And she got wind of it, went to one of the physicians that she knows also is very much in that mindset, and they just had a little freak-out session. Generated a lot of phone calls that zinged right back to me round about through everybody else, and then I heard about it . . .
>
> I thought, well, first of all, this is none of their business. Secondly, it's medically indicated. And thirdly, what are they going to do, fire me? I mean it's just—it was so stupid. But *it just showed that there were differ-*

ences in comfort level about doing these procedures, that some people were very much against them and did not want to know that we were doing a procedure on a live fetus.

For Dr. Kern, this experience brought to light the extent of the restrictions on abortion in her practice. Eventually, when she communicated with her colleague the details of the case, her colleague ultimately agreed with the medical necessity of the abortion, the crisis dissipated, and the situation ended amicably. But, Dr. Kern said, "It was a big effort."

Dr. Dougherty, practicing in the South, shared an experience during which he and his colleague were not able to resolve their differences of opinion, which similarly functioned to teach Dr. Dougherty about the parameters of abortion comfort in his practice culture. As mentioned earlier, Dr. Dougherty never expected to be able to provide any abortions in his southern small town because of the "business climate" around abortion. In the following tragic patient story, he intervened to help refer a patient to get an abortion elsewhere:

> I had a patient, she was around eighteen to twenty weeks pregnant—auto wreck . . . became a quadriplegic. And . . . she had thought about it and prayed about it and talked to her family about it and did not want to continue the pregnancy. And nobody else in my group wanted to talk to her about it.
>
> And when I was on call, I dropped in and I said, "I understand that you're worried about being able to carry this baby to term and all the complications and being able to raise a child"—and her husband was killed and one of her children was killed in the car wreck—clearly, she'd already been through enough emotional upheaval and to make this decision was a tough decision. And I got her referred down to [the university] and they did a D&E on her down there.

Dr. Dougherty found out later that another physician had seen her "to present the other side of the case":

> I went to tell him about another patient, and then he brought it up: "I understand you went by and talked to her about having an abortion, that you were able to get her sent down to [the university]." I'm like, "Yeah." [And he said,] "That's just unfortunate. I tried to go down and talk to her

and talk her out of it because she's taking another life." I said, "Listen, we clearly are going to disagree on this topic and not change our minds about it, so . . . I appreciate your opinion and your side of the story and I expect you to appreciate mine." I'm not going to get into a pissing match and I'm not going to be a flag-waving, pro-choice fanatic in my own practice, but if a patient wants to know the whole story about everything, I'm willing to tell her the whole story.

In light of these experiences of intergroup practice conflict, it is not surprising that several physicians I spoke with advocate for the establishment of clear abortion policies in private practice. Group practices, by definition, share patients. One of the benefits of having a clear policy about abortion is that it can help avert scheduling snafus where one doctor schedules a patient for an abortion, and another, who does not want to perform abortions, happens to be on call and needs to either do the procedure or care for the patient. Dr. Fulton is relieved that the no-abortion policy in her practice is clear to everyone for this reason. "I think having a blanket policy makes it a little easier," she said, "in terms of, this is what we do, boom, that's the end of it and I don't have to really deal with it. You know what I mean? Because I think it'd be difficult if it was someone else's patient. What if it came up on a call day with someone else who didn't do them? It just kind of makes it, I think, messy dealing with other partners."

This exact scenario happened to Dr. Graham and helped her realize that, despite the formality of the abortion policy of her practice, conflict can still arise because doctors differ in their willingness to do even those abortions that are medically and genetically indicated. "I set up a patient for an induction," she said, "a sixteen-week patient who had [a fetal anomaly], and the two partners that were on [call] both don't do inductions, and I didn't even realize they didn't do them for any reason . . . it ended up getting changed to another day, but it brought [to my] attention there are definitely partners who won't do it at all. You really need to communicate if you're going to set something up on somebody else's call day."

Dr. Hayner, practicing in a western small town, opted out of abortion training during residency because of his religious convictions, but he is sympathetic to the need for abortion in some cases. Regardless, he would rather be in a no-abortion practice. He feels that clarifying values and policies around abortions is necessary for those practicing in the ob-gyn field:

> [Abortion] is so much a part of being an ob-gyn that it's important to be up front where you stand on it from the get-go. And I've seen practices that split up because half the partners do 'em and the other half don't. Instead of being undercover about what you believe on it, it's better to be open and up front and say, "Yes I do 'em," or "no I don't" . . . I think it's important to decide where you stand on it, and either pursue a group that is either actively doing them and that you'd fit in, or decide that, "Hey, I'm not going to do 'em" or "I'm going to just do it in a limited manner." And being able to incorporate [that] into your interviewing process [when you are looking for physicians to join the practice].

Opinions differed about how important it was to have a clear abortion policy in order to avoid conflict between colleagues in the work environment. While the clarity and professional civility that abortion policies can offer are valued by Drs. Graham, Fulton, and Hayner, among others I spoke with, Dr. Brill argues the opposite. He looks back fondly on his experience working in a group in a western urban area with no specific abortion policy and a plurality of views and practices concerning it: "The culture of the group was such that it was recognized that when you get twenty ob-gyns together, there's going to be a lot of different ways people are going to be doing stuff. And therefore you by golly better buy into the concept that there's lots of different ways to do it." Dr. Brill's sentiment that there is value in plurality and openness around abortion was shared by some physicians who worked in notoriously liberal areas. Similarly, those physicians in my study who worked in academic environments (residency teaching programs) expected abortion to be tolerated. Ultimately, those working in more liberal political climates enjoyed relatively more freedom to perform abortions if they so wished; the rest endured formal and informal practice constraints with regards to abortion.

The Buck, Passed

Shortly after going into practice, even pro-choice physicians committed to integration in their practices came up against a certain irony presented by the current organizational structure of medical services and the marginalization of abortion care. That is, when doctors practice in small and/or conservative communities where abortion providers are in short supply, they feel too visible and vulnerable to provide abortion. On the other hand, doctors who practice in bigger cities and more liberal areas find that their services are not as desperately needed. Abortion clinics and academic/teaching abortion services fill the void, so it is easy for physicians to forgo struggling with the complexities of abortion practice. Hence, little change is made in the structure of service delivery, the organization of abortion services remains problematic, and the scarcity of abortion providers endures in smaller and/or more conservative communities. Meanwhile, specialized abortion clinics provide 93 percent of the abortions in the United States (Jones et al. 2008), and the stigma, controversy, and violence stay centralized there.

While some physicians leave residency committed to changing this situation, others come to see it as the natural order of things. Dr. Rebecca Holmes spoke about how her residency training in a northeastern urban area taught her that abortions were largely performed in the urban centers and that most private-practice physicians outside of abortion clinics did not tend to take the risks involved in being associated with abortion. "Oh, I knew. It was kind of unspoken," she said. "You just sort of knew because you did your residency, you also rotated among the private hospitals [in the area] your second, third, and fourth year . . . But you were constantly in and around so you knew that out in the suburbs they weren't really doing abortions. [It] wouldn't even be a Catholic hospital, it was just sort of understood that abortions were not performed there." She paused, remembered that one physician in a more elite hospital frequently did abortions for privately insured patients in her suburb, and went on to say:

> But mostly it was [the abortion clinic] in the city. You just kind of understood it. People just didn't take it on. But you also have to understand [that] I trained at the time when someone went into the [abortion clinic] and shot people. So besides the moral thing, people weren't really willing to place themselves at risk from that standpoint. I don't know. It's just one of those things that you just thought to yourself—never literally consciously—"I don't want to place myself in that kind of position." You

just kind of knew. You just sort of understood why everyone else operated kind of quietly about it.

In her northeastern urban area, because of the violence she mentioned, many providers were more concerned about violence than stigma, and, as Dr. Wong, who also practices in this area, said, "Given that we have so many services available . . . [doctors] just feel it's not a headache they want to take on."

Dr. Paz, working in a southern urban area, was initially eager to include abortion in her practice but eventually came to the conclusion that referring out was the better option for her private practice as well:

> I think we have good clinics in [this] area . . . clinics staffed by [residents] and private-practice docs who have done it for a long time . . . although I wanted to do it, the legality of everything started coming up, the whole bombing in Alabama, a lot of the—the wait period, the counseling—a lot of these things started popping up as I went into residency. And so at that point I decided, in order to make the practice run smoother, to just refer these people to these clinics. And I've had a very good experience with these clinics.

Even in cities without a history of activism or violence around abortion, the tendency to refer out abortion services was widespread. The lack of abortion services being offered in private practice normalized the structure of services for new physicians entering the area, in much the same way as it did for Dr. Holmes above. Dr. Radik assessed private practice in the suburbs of her western urban area in the same way. "I don't think that there's a lot of abortions going on," she said. "I mean . . . on the east side here, there's just [two hospitals]. I know all the physicians at [one of them]. They're not doing elective terminations, and I know that nobody here [in our practice] is doing elective terminations except in maybe a rare circumstance. I mean, I think that they're sending most of their terminations to the clinics at this point." Whether or not Dr. Radik is correct in her belief that private practitioners are not doing abortions, her perception that they are all being referred to abortion clinics reinforces her expectations that abortion would be excluded from her own practice, as it likely does for other physicians in her area.

I spoke with three physicians working in different branches of a large nonsectarian, physician-owned, managed-care organization with its own hospital facilities. Each of them told me that abortions were contracted out to abortion clinics. The reasoning for this is officially financial. For cost-effectiveness, this HMO contracts out a variety of highly specialized services that are not done routinely or that require a special technology. Abortion is neither of these things, however; it is both common and low-tech. Regardless, because of the existence of ample low-cost abortion services in the three large urban areas where these HMOs are located, it may well have been equivalent or cheaper for abortion services to be contracted out to them.

Dr. Gail Frank explained why she believes this arrangement is not motivated by antiabortion sentiment. While physicians at this HMO do not routinely do abortions for patients, abortions are not prohibited, and she has performed abortions for her patients under special medical circumstances.

> I wasn't part of this [decision], but at some point [the HMO] decided to contract [abortions] out . . . It's not that we are prohibited from doing them, and I've done a couple . . . but we aren't set up to run a real clinic and do them efficiently. So the ones I have done have been exceptional ones . . . [For example], I did one in a patient who was just diagnosed with breast cancer and had a nine-month-old. And so basically I just did an abortion [and a tubal ligation] to kind of expedite it, because she was starting chemo.

However, Dr. Deena Newirth, another physician working for this HMO, argues that the organization's motivation for contracting out abortion care is not purely financial either. She believes that, much like the no-abortion policies discussed above, the HMO is contracting them out to avoid conflict by passing it on to the abortion clinics in the area:

> [The administration] is so happy to not have to deal with it [abortion]. They're not interested in it . . . the chief of my department told me that very early on. She just told me, "I think everybody's just very relieved that we don't have to worry about this ourselves" . . . And she's somebody who's actually a supporter, but she was relieved as the chief not to have to

deal with [everything]—who was going to do them, who wasn't going to do them, and whether the department had to be all in agreement about providing the service, that kind of thing . . .

I don't know if they're thinking that they don't want to be a target that way, or [they don't want to] have people protesting outside their clinics, or whatever could happen if you start to provide . . . It might just be a relief for them to just say we have these other [folks] do them and Planned Parenthood takes it all, *takes all the flak.*

Contracting out abortion and all of its problems to abortion clinics, this HMO is doing methodically what other medical entities do perhaps inadvertently. Catholic health networks overtly prohibit abortions and end up having the same results, but in a more roundabout way. Such networks operate about 15 percent of all hospital beds in the United States (CHA 2009). They frequently own the buildings where private practices are located near the hospital and impose their abortion restrictions on the renting physicians. Dr. Carrie Becker said that the Catholic health network in her western urban area owns so much of the medical real estate that the graduates of her residency program cannot continue to provide abortions there even though many of them want to:

The majority of our residents stay in town, and we have a very, very strong health-care system that has a lot of tentacles through the community that's a Catholic institution. Even though you have an independent practice, they own the building, and they refuse to allow you to do abortions—even if it's in your own [private] practice . . . That has really impacted a lot of folks in town . . . even though they've wanted to provide, they've joined this practice that then is in this building. The practice isn't Catholic, but the whole area is . . . there're several private groups associated with that facility, and so it makes it really tough.

While the Catholic health networks overtly prohibit abortion for ideological reasons—and not fear of stigma and conflict—the result of their prohibitions, like those of the rest of the medical community, is to funnel abortion patients to the abortion clinics, further consolidating abortion services.

One more reason that abortion is passed on to abortion clinics, beyond controversy, economics, and ideology, is convenience. Some physicians who work in academic centers with no prohibitions whatsoever find that they are inclined to send their patients to the residency abortion service so the patients will be seen more quickly, with less trouble for the physician's schedule. Dr. Claudia Mendez explained:

> Basically in my practice, if I want to do an abortion on one of my patients, I certainly can. Some of my partners do, some don't. But as it turns out, just for the sake of convenience and for the sake of what's easiest for the patient, I think we tend to send them to the hospital [residency abortion service] . . . When the patient needs to be scheduled, you can schedule [her] within two days. As opposed to if I was trying to schedule it for myself at the surgical center it would be a longer waiting period. So I think for that reason, for the patient's convenience, it's better to do it that way . . . if I saw a patient today that wanted to have an abortion, I don't think I have any open spots on my schedule to do anything for a few weeks. And that's not adequate.

The dilemma Dr. Mendez put forth was not uncommon. Once a patient decides she wants an abortion, she often wants to have it done quickly. The timeliness of an abortion procedure, as well as the social and political complexity of it, can make it stand out logistically from other office visits.

Physicians in some states are also deterred by the various requirements of antiabortion legislation. Dr. Graham practices in a western urban area where she thinks it is possible to integrate abortion into private practice, but physicians struggle with the paperwork and waiting periods that are mandated by the state for abortions:

> Some of the bureaucracy that is involved with abortions now, like some of these state requirements and things . . . it's like four pages that you have to fill out and read, and there are certain time requirements, and you have to offer the patients and go to this website and [see] these pictures, and . . . I mean, most of my partners have said, "Well, that's just a pain . . . I'm not even going to bother doing it . . . [the abortion clinics] do this all the time. It's easier just to let them do it."

When I asked physicians how integration would work, a number of them saw scheduling and paperwork as time-consuming obstacles. Some suggested leaving a time slot open every week for abortions, but this plan would entail accepting a certain amount of income loss on the weeks when there were no abortions scheduled. Dr. Anna Lee described the constraints private practitioners face when trying to incorporate abortion into their practices:

> The challenge has been getting the urgent patients, time-sensitive patients in quickly. Most of the time in ambulatory care, the appointments are fixed and set weeks in advance or even months in advance. And when a woman calls for an urgent visit because of pregnancy-related complication, fetal anomaly or an abortion . . . that's very time sensitive. And so the challenge is creating a schedule template that allows for those urgent visits that come in and scheduling enough time to do proper counseling and the procedure in the office.

In addition to figuring out how to allot time for abortion patients in the average private-practice schedule, some doctors worry about having adequate psychological support on hand for abortion patients and the potential emotional discomfort of having prenatal and abortion patients in the office together at the same time.

It is important to note the benefits of specialized abortion services. Their high security, efficiency, and exclusive focus on abortion makes many of these clinics better at providing appropriate counseling and medical care than some physicians might be in their own offices. With few good models of how to do it, the various constraints on physicians seem to lead to the same conclusion: integrating abortion into general practice is hard, and it is no surprise that physicians keep referring their patients to nearby abortion clinics, perpetuating the segregated structure—and the buck-passing—of abortion care.

Summary

Being an abortion provider is highly problematic in many parts of the United States. Physicians noted stigma from discussions with colleagues and community members who used derogatory language and labels such as *abortionist*. And they learned the extent of the contentiousness surrounding abortion through interactions with employers who prohibited abortion practice and colleagues and patients who opposed it. Such interactions were sometimes uncomfortable or even threatening. At other times the interactions consisted of matter-of-fact pronouncements about no-abortion policies in the practices or hospitals where physicians worked. Colleagues told them that abortions were routinely referred out to abortion clinics or that the local hospitals did not allow them. Physicians in smaller cities feared professional failure and social repercussions if they became associated with abortion.

The result of threats, overt abortion prohibitions, and a medical culture of practice that distances itself from abortion is multilevel, institutionalized buck-passing that marginalizes abortion practice. With dedicated abortion clinics performing 93 percent of abortions (Jones et al. 2008), private-practice ob-gyns, even those who left residency committed to including abortion in their practices, by and large do not continue to perform this relatively simple, safe, and common procedure.

The system perpetuates itself in large urban areas with plentiful abortion services. Many physicians refer their patients to abortion clinics even when relatively few barriers to abortion practice exist because it is more convenient for their clinic schedules, faster for the patients, or more cost-effective. The abortion clinics themselves are efficient because abortion is more or less all they do. Hence, the services, paperwork, and counseling for abortion have been streamlined more effectively than they would be in a general ob-gyn clinic setting. At the same time, even in large urban areas, antiabortion violence and conflict around abortion persist. The aforementioned factors motivate private-practice physicians in urban areas and small towns alike to avoid abortion. Ultimately, *willing* and even highly motivated physicians find that the current organization of health care all but prohibits abortion practice within mainstream medicine.

CHAPTER 6

Abortion Prohibitions and Miscarriage Management in Catholic-Owned Health Care

Dr. Brian Smits decided to pursue a fellowship in perinatology when he graduated residency in the late 1990s because male ob-gyns were "just not finding jobs." Female patients had become increasingly interested in having female physicians. But that was not the only reason he decided to subspecialize. "I really enjoyed high-risk obstetrics," he explained, "because it is a little bit of medicine, it's a little bit of surgery. There's a lot of variety so it keeps you from getting bored." When he returned to the East Coast, where he planned to settle down after his fellowship, he found a job in a Catholic hospital. He described himself as a bit "naïve" about the job search process. He had substantial experience doing abortions during his residency and fellowship, but he needed employment and therefore signed a contract with prohibitions on abortion and other reproductive health services. "I took a job which I was a little nervous about," he said, "and I was right. I initially started out at St. Mary's, which is Catholic . . . It was in my contract that if I discussed birth control, abortion, did an abortion, a tubal ligation, then it was grounds for immediate termination of employment, and, you know, 'you will practice your medicine by the guidelines of the Roman Catholic Church' . . . and that's actually what caused me to leave St. Mary's."

Many non-Catholic health practitioners, like Dr. Smits, work in Catholic hospitals in the United States. Catholic hospitals were established in this country during the late nineteenth century, as were Jewish hospitals, to better serve their constituencies in the face of pervasive discrimination. Catholics in particular were concerned about their patients not being able to receive their last rites and being pressured to convert to Protestantism at crisis moments (Starr 1982). But it was not long until both Jewish and Catholic hospitals began to serve people of all faiths (white people, that is; they still denied admission to blacks). Over the past century, a variety of religious hospitals have come to serve and employ people of all denominations and racial and ethnic backgrounds around the United States.

Catholic hospitals have stood out, however, in both their numbers and policies. Nearly 70 percent of religiously affiliated U.S. hospitals are Catholic (Uttley and Pawelko 2002). The Catholic Health Association reports that its members constitute 12.7 percent of the nation's hospitals, operating 15 percent of the nation's hospital beds; and in Washington, D.C., and the twenty-one states where they are most well established, they account for more than one-fifth of hospital admissions (CHA 2009). They are also the largest single group of not-for-profit hospitals in the country (CHA 2009). But unlike the Jewish, Presbyterian, Methodist, and Episcopalian affiliated hospitals, which have generally operated in a nonsectarian manner, posing few or no constraints on patients' abilities to obtain health-care services (Uttley and Pawelko 2002), Catholic hospitals have as their mission "to serve those in need and transform society on behalf of Jesus and the Catholic Church" (Place 1998), which includes requiring that treatment be consistent with "Catholic moral principles"(CHA 2001) through the omission of certain reproductive health and end-of-life services.

Since the 1990s, Catholic health care around the United States has grown tremendously as Catholic-owned hospitals purchased or merged with numerous nonsectarian hospitals (Uttley and Pawelko 2002). The lay press, legal scholars, and social scientists have discussed the effect these mergers have on patient care, particularly women's reproductive health care (Brooks 2006; Fogel and Rivera 2004; Gelb and Shogan 2005; Joyce 2002; Labi 1999; Palley and Kohler 2003; Sloboda 2001; Vitello 2006). This literature has focused largely on Catholic health-care policies prohibiting contraception, tubal ligation, sterilization, emergency contraception, and abortion. Medical journals have shown interest in the broader concerns of a physician's right to refuse, refer, or inform patients of ser-vices to which they have religious objections (Charo 2005; Curlin et al. 2007), but few articles in the medical literature to date have addressed the effect of Catholic hospital policies on patient care and the professional conduct of physicians (Bellandi 1998; Gallagher 1997). Although other hospitals may also restrict or prohibit certain reproductive health services, evaluating the practices of Catholic hospitals is important because of their growth and prominence. In certain regions within the United States, they have become the sole provider (Uttley and Pawelko 2002); hence, millions of patients end up seeking routine and emergency care from such hospi-tals without much prior knowledge about how Catholic religious doctrine may preclude the care they may ultimately want or need.[1]

The restrictions that Catholic hospitals place on reproductive services bothered Dr. Smits, but the catalyst for his quitting came about through an issue that he had, until working in St. Mary's, seen as relatively un-controversial in the world of obstetrics: miscarriage management. As a perinatologist, much of his work revolved around trying to save high-risk pregnancies. But for previable fetuses (less than approximately twenty-three weeks old), little can be done to save the pregnancy if the mem-branes of the amniotic sac are ruptured.[2] After that point, it is only a matter of hours before infection can threaten the health of the pregnant woman. Therefore, using the same procedures by which abortions are performed, the physicians of this study were routinely trained to facili-tate spontaneous abortion (evacuate the contents of the uterus) when a woman showed up at the hospital who was less than twenty-three weeks pregnant, bleeding, and cramping, and had ruptured membranes. This means the pregnancy is over. The woman can either continue to labor as she would in childbirth to deliver the previable (or nonviable) fetus, often with the help of pain and labor-inducing medications, or, if a physician with the appropriate training can be found, the woman can choose a sur-gical procedure in order to expedite spontaneous abortion and to reduce the risk of infection. The surgical procedure in the second trimester typi-cally takes between fifteen and thirty minutes to complete and, in contrast with the hours (or sometimes days) of labor, is often seen as an easier and more comfortable option for a woman experiencing a miscarriage.

A problem arose for Dr. Smits when he took care of a patient whose fetus had not yet died, even though her membranes had ruptured and she was infected and sick. Because the fetus was still alive, the Catholic hospital ethics committee viewed evacuation of the uterus as an abortion, and it would not approve the procedure. Dr. Smits recounted the details of the case: "I had this one situation where—I'll never forget this, it was awful—where I had one of my partners accept this patient at nineteen weeks. And the pregnancy was in the vagina. It was over. But she [the patient] wanted everything done. And so he takes this patient and transferred her to [our] tertiary medical center, which I was just livid about, and, you know, [*sarcastically*] 'We're going to save the pregnancy.'" Dr. Smits was angry because the pregnancy was only nineteen weeks along, and given the extent to which the patient had already begun to expel the pregnancy, there was really no chance of fetal survival. Therefore, he saw the fact that she would occupy a coveted hospital bed and physician care in the tertiary medical center—a specialized center for high-risk pregnancies—as wasteful of time and resources that could be allocated to the management of other precarious but viable pregnancies. He continued:

> So of course, I'm on call when she gets septic, and she's septic to the point that I'm [using medication] to keep her blood pressure up and I have her on a cooling blanket because she's 106 degrees. And I needed to get everything out [of the uterus]. And so I put the ultrasound machine on and there was still a heartbeat, and [the hospital ethics committee] wouldn't let me [do the procedure] because there was still a heartbeat. And this woman is dying before our eyes.

Dr. Smits's ethics committee wanted him to wait until the fetus's heart had stopped to approve his request to evacuate the uterus. Until this moment, Dr. Smits had viewed his hospital's abortion prohibition as primarily affecting his ability to offer abortions to patients with fetal anomalies or medical contraindications with pregnancy—patients he would then need to refer to abortion clinics elsewhere.[3] But in this emergency situation, his patient's life was seriously threatened because of the policy. Such a disjuncture between what he considered to be the standard of care in miscarriage management and what was acceptable to his hospital's ethics committee was both surprising and frightening to him.

Maternal Health Exemption

Does the Catholic Church provide for a maternal health exemption? The answer to this question is not straightforward, and it is not one I was intending to research at the outset of this study. But Dr. Smits's story is one of several related stories that emerged during my interviews. I had no questions planned about miscarriage management per se; I was more interested in how doctors dealt with abortion for elective, genetic, or medical indications and had not yet seen how miscarriages could be controversial for physicians. However, more than one-third of the doctors I interviewed worked in Catholic hospitals, either full time or on occasion. Most of these individuals had little to no experience doing abortions after residency. But for some, miscarriage management was what immediately came to mind when I asked them whether they had ever had conflicts with colleagues over abortion. Halfway through my data collection I saw the trend and started asking about it directly.[4] It became clear that this is an issue where the politics of abortion play out in the Catholic hospital; where the value of fetal life is measured against maternal life; and where the pope's decree concerning abortion starkly challenges modern medical practice.[5]

These are not new issues to the world of Catholic health care. The earlier part of the twentieth century witnessed stringent abortion policies with no maternal life exemption at all. The nuns and priests governing medical practice in Catholic hospitals held the position on abortion that was articulated by Bishop Spaulding in 1869: "The murder of an infant before its birth is, in the sight of God and His Church, as great a crime, as would be the killing of a child after birth . . . No mother is allowed, under any circumstances to permit the death of her unborn infant, not even for the sake of preserving her own life" (Mohr 1978: 186). Finding the same sentiment in her historical research, Leslie Reagan documents debate between a Catholic priest and physicians holding a symposium on abortion sponsored by the Chicago Medical Society in 1904 (Reagan 1997). The priest argued that abortion was not justified even "when absolutely necessary to save the mother," to which one physician responded: "With 'the advance of moral feeling, the opinion has developed that . . . where the lives of both mother and child are imperiled and one can be saved, the child should be sacrificed, since the value of the mother to the State is far greater than that of the unborn babe'" (Reagan 1997: 63). Emphasizing the increasing distance between medical and religious understandings on the issue, a second physician at the symposium commented, "Reasoning that may satisfy the conscience of a theologian does not satisfy the conscience of the physician" (Reagan 1997: 63).

The issue came to a head in 1920 when five non-Catholic physicians resigned from Marquette University Medical School, a Jesuit institution. The physicians quit when the university's president intervened to ensure enforcement of the strict abortion prohibition within the hospital. Upon quitting, one doctor declared, "I know of no other sect in the country that takes the stand that the unborn child cannot be destroyed if the life of the mother is at stake" (Joyce 2002: 107).

In the aftermath of this unflattering publicity, while heading the newly founded Catholic Hospital Association,[6] a Jesuit priest named Charles Moulinier launched a campaign to mainstream and standardize Catholic hospitals through affiliation with the American College of Surgeons in 1921. This was accomplished despite Catholic infighting and lent a great degree of credibility to Catholic health care in the United States. Kathleen Joyce, a historian of Catholic health care in the twentieth century, argues that Catholic leaders achieved this with a compromise. As unpopular and unlikely as Catholic compromise has been around abortion, she argues that indeed "many Catholic hospital leaders calculated that it *could* be lawful to mute condemnation of practices their church deemed evil in the pursuit of a greater good" (Joyce 2002: 93). The "greater good" for these actors would be the survival of Catholic health care. Joyce writes, "Downplaying controversial teachings bought Catholic hospitals the time they needed to establish themselves as an integral part of the modern health care system" (Joyce 2002: 111).

By 1948, emboldened by the financial strength of their hospitals as well as medical advances that made it possible for most women with health problems to carry their pregnancies to term (Joyce 2002), Catholic health leaders became more vocal about their stance on abortion. At this time, the first formal and detailed code of Catholic medical policy was written entitled "Ethical and Religious Directives for Catholic Health Care Services" (CHA 2001).[7] This document calls for variations on mainstream medical practice largely in the dealings of Catholic health services with care at the beginning and ending of life. In terms of reproductive health care, the directives prohibit birth control, infertility treatment, sterilization, and abortion, and sanction only prenatal care and natural family planning (CHA 2001).

Over the next few decades Catholic leaders continually debated and revised the directives in response to what they saw as undesirable changing attitudes and regionally specific liberalized interpretation of laws regarding sterilization and contraception. By 1994, several Catholic organizations, theologians, and ethicists working together finished revising the directives for strictly standardized national use (O'Rourke, Kopfen-Steiner, and Hamel 2001). An important qualification of the abortion prohibition was articulated in this version of the directives, which was an expanded version that included detailed treatment of a variety of ethical issues arising with the advancement of medical and reproductive technologies (O'Rourke, Kopfen-Steiner, and Hamel 2001). The qualification, Directive 47, concludes that if the pregnant woman is at risk, termination of the pregnancy is allowable: "Operations, treatments, and medications that have as their direct purpose the cure of a proportionately serious pathological condition of a pregnant woman are permitted when they cannot be safely postponed until the unborn child is viable, even if they will result in the death of the unborn child" (CHA 2001).

Thus, Directive 47 indicates that the death of the fetus can be permitted only as a secondary outcome of the steps taken to preserve the health or the life of the pregnant woman. Because of vague wording, the distinction between "health" and "life" is unclear. The issue at hand is to some extent "intention." As long as the intention is to treat the woman, not the fetus, the outcome of the fetal death is technically tolerable under Catholic doctrine under the law of "double effect." This law allows for action toward a good end in certain circumstances when the action is known to cause a bad result in the process. Specifically applying the way that double effect is used in obstetrical matters, ethicist David Solomon writes:

> The Catholic magisterium has argued that the principle allows one to distinguish morally among cases where a pregnancy may need to be ended in order to preserve the life of the mother. The principle is alleged to allow the removal of a life-threatening cancerous uterus, even though this

procedure will bring the death of a fetus, on the grounds that in this case the death of the fetus is not "directly" intended. The principle disallows cases, however, in which a craniotomy (the crushing of the fetus's skull) is required to preserve a pregnant woman's life, on the grounds that here a genuine evil, the death of the fetus, is "directly" intended.

Pointing to a lack of consensus in the world of Catholic health care, Solomon continues:

> There is significant disagreement, even among those philosophers who accept the principle, about the cogency of this application. Some philosophers and theologians . . . argue that the greater value attaching to the pregnant woman's life makes even craniotomy morally acceptable. Others fail to see a morally significant difference between the merely "foreseen" death of the fetus in the cancerous uterus case and the "directly" intended death in the craniotomy case.[8]

In an attempt to bring clarity to the management of spontaneous abortion given the inconclusiveness of this debate over maternal versus fetal life, shortly after the 1994 edition of the directives was released, an explicit discussion of the treatment of previable miscarriage cases was featured in *Health Progress: The Official Journal of the Catholic Health Association of the United States*. The following text was published in order to define protocol for physicians practicing in a Catholic hospital who manage miscarriage when the fetus has not yet expired: "Too often, well-meaning but uninformed observers claim that all interventions resulting in fetal death constitute a direct, and therefore prohibited, abortion. Such an appraisal often is based on the erroneous conclusion that the term 'abortion' conveys only and always a moral assessment. Such a conclusion is evidence of a lack of precision in understanding both moral and medical terminology" (deBlois and O'Rourke 1995: 38). Because the Catholic Church is firmly opposed to the termination of human life—which includes fetal life and extrauterine life, as in cases of euthanasia or suicide—the writer is trying to bring a nuanced understanding to situations in which one life is pitted against another, where the two lives may have opposing needs. He cautions against condemnation of abortion when there is a medically complex situation where abortion may be necessary to save the mother's life. He goes on to present to the physician readers the case management of a patient very similar to that of Dr. Smits:

> A 23-year-old woman is admitted to the emergency department with abdominal cramps and fever. She is 19 weeks pregnant, and fetal heart tones are present. Cervical membranes are bulging, and amniotic fluid is leaking. The cervix is dilated 2 to 3 cm, and fetal parts are palpable through the cervix. After appropriate consultation, the diagnosis of "probable uterine infection and threatened abortion" is made.[9]
>
> The physician makes reasonable efforts to sustain the pregnancy and treat the infection, but with little success. The physician recommends artificial rupture of the membranes and drug-induced labor. (deBlois and O'Rourke 1995: 39)

What the writer considers to be "reasonable efforts" to save the pregnancy is not entirely clear and remains up to the discretion of the physician or the ethics committee. In the analysis of the case management, the writer invokes Directive 47:

> Directive 47 is helpful here, primarily because it emphasizes that the moral judgment in such a case requires adequate medical data. In addition, though Directive 47 does not spell out the terms of the assessment, it does indicate briefly the manner in which the assessment should be done.
>
> Reviewing the case in the light of the directive, we can draw the following conclusions:
>
> - The physicians performed the intervention (membrane rupture and induction of labor) so they could empty the patient's uterus of its contents, treat the infection, and complete a labor process that, although it was ineffective, had already begun.
> - To induce labor, the physicians used the only drug that would alleviate the patient's pathological condition, the uterine infection. The drug helped cure the infection (a treatment that was directly intended) and brought on delivery of a previable fetus (an outcome that was not directly intended).
> - Fetal survival was not possible in this case because of the worsening uterine infection. Moreover, inevitable abortion was indicated by the protruding fetal part.
> - The resulting fetal death was indirect. (deBlois and O'Rourke 1995: 39)

From a close examination of both Directive 47 and the analysis of its application during previable spontaneous abortion in the above article, it appears that this Catholic health directive can be construed to endorse the accepted interventions for miscarrying patients; that is, it endorses uterine evacuation when there is no hope of saving the pregnancy because excessive delay in doing so is dangerous for the pregnant woman. The question remains, however: what happened with Dr. Smits's case? Did his hospital's ethics committee not agree with the above interpretation of Directive 47? Did it not understand it, or not know about it? Were there problems in communication between Dr. Smits and the committee about the patient? It is hard to know without having been there to observe the events that took place. Nevertheless, the similar stories my interviews unearthed in different areas of the United States indicate that Dr. Smits is not unique in his experience and that Catholic hospitals have not reached complete consensus on these issues.

There may be disagreement among Catholic hospital ethics committees about how long the physician should wait to intervene. If the pregnancy is unsalvageable (membranes broken, bleeding, visible fetal parts), does the physician need to stall treatment until the fetus dies? How great a risk to the pregnant woman's health will be tolerated while treatment is on hold? Does the patient need to be infected, at risk for sepsis, before the ethics committee will approve evacuation of the uterus in Catholic hospitals? And of what relevance are the patient's preferences in this scenario?

Discussions I had with physicians managing such miscarriage cases in Catholic hospitals indicated that confusion or disagreement about how to interpret the directives exists nationally both at individual (practitioner) and institutional (hospital ethics committee) levels. Doctors spoke of their frustration at not being able to terminate a pregnancy when they judged it appropriate. Essentially, these physicians felt they had unsatisfactory choices. They could (1) transport the patient to a non-Catholic facility where the evacuation of the uterus is permitted, (2) postpone treatment of the patient until the fetus dies, or (3) disregard the ethics committee's authority, risking their own job or professional reputation, in order to perform the prohibited procedure. I found that physicians did all three of these things and did not feel particularly good about any of them.

Delaying Care and Transporting Patients

Dr. Mary White, a physician working in a midwestern Catholic hospital, summarized the situation at her hospital: approval for termination is rare when a fetal heartbeat is present.

> There is an ethics committee that will meet. If the woman is bleeding out [hemorrhaging from the uterus] they may possibly let us do it [the abortion], you know, if it looks like she's going to die if we don't do it, and that's probably our only thing. Because I've had early—you know, people are bleeding, they're all the way dilated, they're only seventeen weeks [pregnant] and "still [a] heartbeat." So we've had to send them . . . to [the university hospital] instead of let them sit here forever and get [an] infection.

Dr. Tiffany Howell, an ob-gyn from the same Catholic hospital in the Midwest, also had to send her patient on a ninety-mile ambulance drive to the university hospital because the ethics committee refused to grant approval:

> She was very early, fourteen weeks. [She] came in . . . and there was a hand sticking out of the cervix. Clearly, the membranes had ruptured and she was trying to deliver . . . There was a heart rate and [we called] the ethics committee and they [said], "Nope, can't do anything." So we had to send her to [the university hospital] . . . You know, these things don't happen that often, but from what I understand it, it's pretty clear. Even if mom is very sick, you know, potentially life-threatening, [you] can't do anything.

Physicians found transports to be a quicker and safer way to procure uterine evacuation in some cases, rather than waiting for fetal death in the Catholic hospital while trying to stave off infection and excessive blood loss. These two cases were the first ones I heard about, and given that they involved the same hospital, I wondered whether that hospital's ethics committee was particularly strict or whether perhaps it was the more conservative environment of the Midwest that brought about such policies. Soon after these interviews, however, I spoke with a physician in a liberal western city who encountered similar transports from the Catholic hospital into her own nonsectarian one. Dr. Carrie Becker received a request to accept the transfer of a very sick miscarrying patient from a Catholic hospital. In this case, the patient had already become septic. When Dr. Becker received the request, she recommended that the physician from the Catholic hospital perform a D&C there and not delay her care with the transport:

> Because the fetus was still alive, they wouldn't intervene. And she was hemorrhaging and they called me and wanted to transport her, and I said, "It sounds like she's unstable, and it sounds like you need to take care of her there"—and I was on a recorded line, I reported them as an EMTALA (Emergency Medical Treatment and Active Labor Act) violation[10]—And the physician [said], "This isn't something that we can take care of." And I [said], "Well, if I don't accept her, what are you going to do with her?" [He answered], "We'll put her on a floor, we'll transfuse her as much as we can, and we'll just wait 'til the fetus dies."

Ultimately, in order to spare the miscarrying patient unnecessary harm and suffering, Dr. Becker accepted the transfer. She felt the transport was a form of "patient dumping," as the patient lacked health insurance, was denied treatment, and then was transported while unstable. Dr. Becker also saw the suggestion of performing multiple blood transfusions to deal with her blood loss and infection as bad medical practice. Good medical practice, in her view, would have been to surgically empty the contents of the patient's uterus to complete the miscarriage, the source of the infection.

With the conversation on record, the Catholic hospital responded by reprimanding the physician who transferred the patient. Catholic officials also told Dr. Becker that their policy would be changing in order to leave more discretion to doctors about when to intervene in spontaneous abortions. But a few months later, Dr. Becker received a similar call to transport to her hospital a patient with a pulmonary embolism who needed an abortion. Pulmonary embolism is a life-threatening condition that can be caused by pregnancy and is considered a medical indication for terminating the pregnancy. While this transport patient may not have been as highly unstable as Dr. Becker's prior one, it demonstrated that this Catholic hospital was not doing terminations for even life-threatening medical indications.

Dealing with Ethics Committees . . . or Not

Dr. Francine Gray, working in a Catholic hospital in the South, shared the story of a case in which a transport patient's miscarriage was already in progress. During residency, Dr. Gray had opted out of abortion training because of her Catholic background. She described herself as somewhat sympathetic to abortion rights—because of the tragedies that occurred before abortion was legal—but she felt morally uncomfortable performing the procedure herself. During our interview she criticized Catholic prohibitions on birth control and abortion for medical or genetic reasons. Interestingly, of all the doctors I spoke with, she seemed the least intimidated (almost cavalier) in her dealings with the hospital ethics committee. "I understand it and I know the rules," she said casually, "because I actually am Catholic. So I really haven't run into too much stuff [when] I would wonder what their philosophy would be."

In the following case Dr. Gray was working in a midsized southern city when a pregnant woman was transferred into her care presenting with chorioamnionitis, a bacterial infection that can lead to serious complications for the mother and the fetus. Like Dr. Smits's patient, Dr. Gray's patient had been transferred to her hospital for its superior facilities for high-risk pregnancy and childbirth. And like Dr. Smits, Dr. Gray felt that the transport was unjustified because there was no real chance of fetal survival.

Unjustified patient transport is a recurring theme in medicine, but unlike most EMTALA cases, where patients are transported for the inability to pay, cases of wrongly transporting patients to higher-level facilities can happen because the treating physician is out of treatment ideas and does not want to be the bearer of bad news. At other times, the physician believes the transport might really help, but the patient gets worse during transport. Similar to the tensions during end-of-life care in the United States (Kaufman 2005; Timmermans 1999), the additional element of grief with fetal loss may make physicians more likely to try to prolong attempts to salvage a pregnancy, even if they are medically and financially unsound.

When Dr. Gray received her already infected patient, she was concerned for the patient's life and future fertility, so she requested approval from the Catholic hospital's ethics committee to use drugs to induce contractions and expedite termination of the pregnancy. "I futzed around for forty-five minutes or so on the phone [with the priest from the ethics committee], trying to get permission to use an induction agent to deliver her because she was sick," she said. "She already had a fever and was sick. Well, they [wouldn't give] me permission because there was a heartbeat, but basically what ended up happening . . . by the time I got to the lady and even got an okay to go ahead with an induction, she actually delivered . . . It was a moot point." Dr. Gray commented that in most cases, the body works hard to expel a pregnancy when feverish or under duress as a survival mechanism. This was one of those cases, and fortunately for the patient, the expulsion was quick, but the process can be lengthy, painful, and sometimes dangerous without medical intervention.

Months later, Dr. Gray encountered another memorable miscarriage. This time, however, she acted differently. She independently decided to *not* consult the ethics committee and to *not* check for a fetal heartbeat so that she could quickly complete the miscarriage. This led to conflict with the nurse assisting her, who either had stronger feelings about the sanctity of fetal life than Dr. Gray or was more committed to practicing medicine by the book (the Catholic book):

> She was fourteen weeks [pregnant] and the membranes were literally out of the cervix and hanging in the vagina. And so with her, I could just take care of it in the ER, but her cervix wasn't open enough . . . so we went to the operating room and the nurse kept asking me, "[Were] there heart tones, [were] there heart tones?" I said, "I don't know, I don't know." Which I kind of knew there would be. But she said, "Well, did you check?" . . . I said, "I don't need an ultrasound to tell me that it's inevitable, the membranes are hanging out of the cervix . . . you can just put [on the paperwork], 'the heart tones weren't documented' and then they can interpret that however they want to interpret that." . . . I said, "Throw it back at me . . . I'm not going to order an ultrasound. It's silly" . . . it would have muddied the water in this case . . .

Why was Dr. Gray less concerned about following ethics committee protocol in this case than in the prior one? Possibly because the case was much less "visible," as the patient had walked into the emergency room and had not been managed by other physicians before Dr. Gray saw her. Essentially, Dr. Gray had fewer individuals looking over her shoulder. Her first patient, on the other hand, had been transported by another physician from another hospital and was further into the pregnancy, which generates more discussion about the possibility of being able to stall labor long enough for the fetus to be born viable. With these differences in mind, the latter case seemed less problematic to Dr. Gray.

She was confident about how she managed this miscarriage, although she was a bit troubled by the conflict with the nurse. When I asked her what she thought would have happened if she had checked for fetal heart tones (or "muddied the waters"), she asked: "[What was I supposed to] do with this lady, just send her home? . . . If I had put her on bed rest, nothing probably would have happened for weeks and weeks and weeks . . . And she was only fourteen weeks, so you know, it's like, what's the chance of getting her to twenty-five [weeks] and then she has to have a premature baby? So anyway, it worked out. I kind of knew better."

Dr. Gray's response here is interesting on a few levels. The fact that she launched into this mental exercise of what would happen to a fourteen-week pregnancy on bed rest is indicative of the unique Catholic culture of obstetrical practice and harks back several decades to a time when a remote chance of fetal life (or none at all) would justify exceptional discomfort and risk to maternal life in the Catholic hospital. In the medical literature, ruptured membranes at fourteen weeks mean only one thing: spontaneous abortion is inevitable. Intravenous antibiotics might be able to delay infection for a while, but eventually the uterus would start prolonged cramping to expel the fetus and placental tissue. Such cramping with bleeding can last for an unpredictable amount of time, with continued risk of infection or hemorrhage, and that is why patients frequently undergo surgical uterine evacuation, which, especially early in the pregnancy, is quick and very safe.

Returning to Dr. Smits, his concerns were comparatively straightforward compared with those of Dr. Gray. He needed to save the life of his miscarrying, now dying patient. His attempts to gain approval for uterine evacuation from the ethics committee had failed, so like Dr. Gray, he took matters into his own hands: "And so I went in to examine her, and I was able to find the umbilical cord through the membranes and just snapped the umbilical cord and . . . 'Oh look. No heartbeat. Let's go.' And she was so sick she was in the ICU for about ten days and very nearly died. And I said, you know, I can't do this. I just can't do this. I can't put myself behind this. This is not worth it to me." And so he quit his job at the Catholic hospital and joined a secular academic medical center.

When I asked Dr. Smits how the hospital administration and ethics committee had responded to the bad medical outcome of the case, he told me they saw it as a problem of a "bad transport": "Nobody thought that the hospital did anything wrong. I think that the biggest issue was that they took this nineteen-weeker on transfer . . . They just said that she didn't need to be in a tertiary medical center . . . The point is that for a nineteen-week pregnancy, you're not going to be able to do anything to save the pregnancy anyway." When I asked what ultimately happened to the patient, he said: "She was in DIC, which means that her coagulation profile was just all out of whack.[11] So they bleed internally. And her bleeding was so bad that the sclera, the whites of her eyes, were red, filled with blood . . . She actually had pretty bad pulmonary disease and wound up being chronically oxygen-dependent, and as far as I know, [she] still is, years later. But, you know, she's really lucky to be alive."

Strategic Communication: Getting Approval

Presumably, Catholic ethics committees vary to some extent among institutions, even if their decisions are based on the same doctrine. As we saw in the interpretation of Directive 47 for spontaneous abortion, there is room for discretion about what one considers "reasonable attempts to save the pregnancy." Some physicians have success navigating their ethics committees strategically without having to resort to violating hospital protocol, as in the cases of Dr. Smits and Dr. Gray. Dr. John Brill, an ob-gyn working in a Catholic hospital in the rural West, said he was able to get approval in such cases by presenting patients to his ethics committee using the language of the directives strategically. According to the wording and recommended interpretation of Directive 47, uterine evacuation is theoretically legitimate when abortion is inevitable or when the pregnant woman's life is at risk. Dr. Brill demonstrated how two similar cases were handled differently by him and a more religious colleague in part because of the way they interpreted the language of Directive 47:

> I had a woman who was dilated but her placenta was also separating from the inside of the uterus. That's called a placental abruption. And she was right about twenty weeks. And she wanted just to get it over with. And the way I framed the conversation [to the ethics committee] was . . . "She was not interested in trying to prolong this pregnancy. It's all run amok, the placenta is separating, and the other maternal concern that we have is that if we continue to watch this placental abruption, it could end up being dangerous to her life, requiring transfusions, or potentially even [causing] maternal death, if left untreated. Even though the fetus still had a heartbeat." And with that, the arguments that center around maternal benefits are persuasive.

The ethics committee approved his request to surgically evacuate the uterus, and Dr. Brill noted that everything "worked out well for everyone," although it "required jumping through hoops." Nonetheless, he found his committee members were sympathetic and concerned about the health risks of delay to the pregnant woman.

He contrasted this case with a similar one managed by another physician in his hospital. He found their approaches to miscarriage management notably distinct, with significant consequences for the patient:

> I've seen Catholic physicians or fundamental Christian physicians make medical decisions that I thought were not in the best interest of the patient but were in line with their interpretations of the Bible . . . I can think of another specific circumstance where a very similar presentation [to the one above]—the physician attempted to stop the labor and to keep her pregnant—and she continued to bleed. And she ended up requiring a transfusion and then losing the pregnancy spontaneously a week or two later. But by then the physician felt like his conscience was clean because it happened the way it was going to happen. My interpretation of it was . . . she got a transfusion that she didn't need to have.

Both patients ultimately recovered safely from their miscarriages, but the latter spent much longer in the medical system with more intervention and the additional risks of transfusion. Clearly, Dr. Brill was critical of his colleague's management of his case. These two cases demonstrate how different interpretations of "reasonable attempts to save the pregnancy" can play out differently in similar patients in the same Catholic hospital governed by the same ethics committee and religious doctrine.

Dr. Brill had advice about how to avoid a bad miscarriage outcome in a Catholic system—how wording and emphasis can make a difference:

> What you end up calling it is . . . an inevitable abortion, where the cervix is open, the woman is bleeding, and there's either placenta or amniotic membrane that's visible at the external os [the outermost opening of the cervix]. You can call that an inevitable abortion. Even with a fetal heart rate, if the conversation is framed about potential maternal complications, that's the argument that can win the day . . .
>
> I learned a good bit of advice actually . . . from the sister that sits on the ethics committee. The first time I tried to have one of these conversations with her, she said, "Well, what are you concerned about with the mom?" . . . Since that time, that's just the way that the conversation gets started . . . I don't know if she was trying to give me a hint or whether she was . . . just interested in doing what she really considers to be the right thing, the moral thing . . . but it certainly helped me out.

Dr. Brill appeared to have a much stronger grasp on navigating the ethics committee in his hospital than others I spoke with who felt it was out of their control. But variability in ethics committees might better explain the different decisions they hand down. The nun who gave advice to Dr. Brill may have simply been moderate in her interpretation of Catholic doctrine and therefore helpful to his cases.

Conclusion

Discussing the effect of books and films that came out in the mid-twentieth century with shocking scenarios of maternal death under Catholic health care,[12] Kathleen Joyce writes:

> The image of a dying woman, pregnant, her life held in the balance as physicians and priests consider the theologically correct clinical response

to her medical crisis, is a wrenching example of some of the questions raised by the Catholic church's involvement in health care. The number of women whose pregnancies demand this sort of life-or-death decision making is, and always has been, proportionately low, but throughout the twentieth century, Catholic teachings on abortion nevertheless have forced the question: How can Catholic hospitals claim, as they have throughout the twentieth century, to be medical institutions committed to the same professional standards and offering the same standard of patient care as the best of their non-Catholic counterparts and, at the same time, allow their own sectarian religious beliefs to prevent doctors from providing lawful, medically appropriate, life-saving treatment? (Joyce 2002: 92)

Joyce's question about the standard of care offered by Catholic hospitals resonates in the current context of the numerous hospital mergers that have thrown highly utilized reproductive services to the wayside. My findings about miscarriage management further this point to a surprising degree. While these data cannot describe how widespread the problem of delay and transport is, they nonetheless indicate that Catholic medical practices reflect confusion and disagreement about how far to extend the Catholic Church's prohibition of abortion. Most Americans know that Catholicism forbids abortion per se, but few would expect that under Catholic health care, uterine evacuation may be prohibited even in cases of inevitable miscarriage.

Catholic doctrine provides a maternal life exemption to the abortion prohibition via Directive 47, but it is unclear how much risk to a patient's life must be present before it is applied. In the physicians' stories presented here, it appears that Catholic hospitals subjected miscarrying pregnant women to more delays in treatment than they would have experienced in other hospitals, and such delays were justified by Catholic doctrine—a doctrine to which many of their patients and doctors do not necessarily subscribe. The medico-religious management of these miscarriages raises questions: What care can pregnant women expect in these situations? What level of discomfort brought about by transports and delays in care is acceptable to the public in order to satisfy the doctrinal needs of these institutions?

Fortunately, with the exception of Dr. Smits's patient, who suffered permanent physical damage because of her experience, the other women we heard about here did not experience detrimental physical outcomes due to the delays in their care. More research is needed to assess whether Catholic hospitals indeed deliver care with higher rates of maternal morbidity than other institutions. Most likely, the effects of this problem on patients are predominantly social and psychological—effects that are hard to measure through the medical outcome data collected from hospitals. Having care delayed while giving false hope about the survival of a pregnancy not only is ethically problematic, but also betrays the widely accepted value of informed consent in medical care. Clearly, one cannot expect the experience of pregnancy loss to be pleasant, but it appears that the experience can be worsened by how religious doctrine affects the running of a Catholic hospital.

The cases reviewed in this chapter go further than to demonstrate a questionable medical practice under Catholic health care. They show what can happen when abortion is prohibited as an inflexible rule or mandate. The structure that privileges the ethics committees' decisions also disempowers physicians from using their individual judgment in particular cases. As we saw in the mid-twentieth century, this is precisely why the directives were codified so clearly, so that the Catholic Church could stem any liberalization in practice patterns arising locally. However, Catholic institutions are more accountable than ever for the particularities of their policies because they now serve more patients (Catholic and non-Catholic) than ever, and as they merge with and take over other hospitals, they promise the communities they serve a comparable standard of care. Furthermore, because the American public holds more liberalized notions regarding abortion, contraception, and sterilization than Catholic leaders, based on the high utilization of these services, Catholic institutions continue to pass the buck to non-Catholic facilities to follow through with the needed and desired care. Is this responsible medicine? At best, the prohibition of such services adds to the societal stigma attached to abortion, contraception, and sexuality in general. At worst, we can look to Dr. Smits's patient as an example of what modern medicine looks like with its hands tied.

CHAPTER 7

Conclusion

At the beginning of this book I asked, What happened to Dr. Chasey's resi-
dents after he trained them in abortion care? Dr. Chasey had spent most
of his career as the director of a midwestern residency's hospital-based
abortion service. He wished, aloud, that his residents had the courage (or
"guts," as he put it) to face the challenges of providing abortion and that
they would continue doing so throughout their careers. But they did not,
and ultimately, most of them stopped providing abortions after residency
(except for the rare genetically or medically indicated exception) for fear
of professional repercussions stemming from abortion stigma, contention
in their communities, and/or restrictions placed on abortion by medical
groups, hospitals, HMOs, or religiously affiliated institutions where they
practiced.

Throughout this book, I have attempted to explain why abortion practice in the United States is so vulnerable to the social and political contention surrounding it and how we have arrived at a place in time where
restrictions on physician autonomy in general, and abortion practice in
particular, are widely tolerated by the medical profession. During the
more than thirty-five years that women have possessed the right to have
an abortion, Americans have generally believed that physicians held a cor-
responding right to provide it. Abortion provision has thus been perceived
as a personal choice. But any good sociologist would caution against explaining a growing trend in the decline of abortion providers as simply
the outcome of a series of personal choices. Joining biography and history
(Mills 1959), I have situated the experiences of new physicians within their

138

structural contexts and found that their personal choices around abortion practice are seriously constrained.

By tracing the history of American medicine's relationship to abortion over the past 150 years, I showed how major medical associations have generally been interested in abortion turf when it served the professionalization project of medicine. During the late nineteenth century, the physicians' crusade against abortion was crucial in criminalizing the procedure as well as in establishing physicians as both moral and medical authorities. The crusade effectively displaced other types of health practitioners competing for medical territory and established these physicians as legitimate guardians of normative sexual and reproductive behavior. This newfound legitimacy also enabled physicians to determine what exact indications made abortion justifiable; these parameters showed some flexibility during the Depression, when unwanted pregnancy was seen as especially detrimental to families, but were tightened during the 1940s and 1950s, when hostility to female independence was widespread. The tightening led to decreased access to safe abortion at the same time that major shifts in sexual culture led to a more noticeable and intolerable public health problem of abortion-related maternal mortality.

Some physician activists and progressive associations (ACOG and APHA) were instrumental in abortion policy change during the 1960s and 1970s; however, many physicians worried about becoming "mere technicians" as abortion became an elective procedure decided upon by only the patient. After legalization, the AMA and many crucial medical bodies were inconsistent and silent on how abortion should be practiced. In their institutional passivity and ambivalence, they failed to incorporate abortion into mainstream medicine. Instead, freestanding abortion clinics proliferated to meet the high demand for abortions while those performed in hospitals steadily declined. Fewer and fewer abortion clinic doctors provided the lion's share of abortions. In the decades after legalization, the marginalization of abortion from mainstream medicine became increasingly problematic as abortion clinics were plagued with harassment, violence, and legislative hurdles from a strong antiabortion movement. In response, abortion rights advocates called for physicians to mainstream abortion by integrating it into their general practices in order to decrease the stigma, visibility, and professional marginalization of abortion care and to counter a growing shortage in abortion providers in many parts of the country.

Physicians, however, appear slow to heed the call. Given that ob-gyns are considered experts of the uterus, that abortion is the third most common procedure their patients of reproductive age will undergo, and that most of these physicians heard the "integration" message during abortion training, I asked whether physicians felt responsible to help ameliorate the growing provider shortage. I found that the lack of a clear professional or legal mandate to provide abortion, as well as the hostile conditions surrounding it, mediates their sense of duty to continue performing abortions after residency. While nearly all of the physicians I interviewed identify themselves as pro-choice, the extent to which they felt professionally obligated to provide abortion varied widely. Ultimately, a physician's sense of professional obligation does not necessarily indicate whether that physician will perform abortions after residency. Likewise, a physician's medical practice often does not reflect his or her individual support for abortion. And while a high degree of politicization is necessary to overcome obstacles to abortion provision, even the most politicized physicians are frequently hindered by geographic, professional, and personal priorities that trump their involvement with abortion care.

Further teasing apart ideology and practice, I explored the moral complexity of learning how to do, doing, and having abortions through the story of Dr. Rina Anderson, whose own pregnancy caused her personal and professional lives to intersect. Her story incorporated an examination of abortion training and techniques, as well as the perspectives of unwilling physicians who partially participated in abortion training. The case of Dr. Anderson served to elucidate moral tensions in abortion work—in particular, how physicians navigated abortion training and practice when their own emotions regarding abortion were not nearly as black and white as abortion rhetoric.

In order to explain why physicians' moral, political, and professional commitments to provide abortion did not always translate into actual provision, I examined the range of barriers that stopped *willing* physicians from incorporating abortion into their practices. Through interactions with colleagues and patients, physicians learned that abortion was not only highly stigmatized and professionally destructive, but that formal and informal policies prohibiting abortion practice would affect them at various levels. Some group practices and hospitals, including Catholic-owned hospitals, had overt abortion prohibitions, while others had a culture of practice that routinely discouraged abortion and encouraged referring patients to abortion clinics in order to maintain civility when hostility toward abortion was present or anticipated. Physicians who practiced in rural or conservative parts of the country especially feared negative consequences such as violence, professional isolation, and loss of business if they became involved with abortion. Some large HMOs contracted out their abortion care to abortion clinics to save money. And physicians in liberal urban areas with no abortion prohibitions often referred patients to the clinics for convenience, in part because the clinics in those areas were efficient and competent and could accommodate patients in a more timely manner. Together, these barriers served to funnel abortion patients to freestanding abortion clinics and continue what I have termed here as the *institutionalized buck-passing* of abortion care in mainstream medicine.

The Catholic-owned health system is the largest (and most inadvertent) institutional buck-passer of reproductive health care. Having come to operate about one-sixth of all hospital beds in the United States, Catholic-owned health care serves and employs Catholics and non-Catholics alike. Because physicians are required upon employment to sign paperwork pledging to practice medicine according to the health doctrine of the Catholic Church, the doctors in my study who worked for Catholic-owned hospitals and groups found that they had no choice about whether to include abortion in their practices because it was firmly prohibited, along with all medicine related to contraception and fertility. Six of the thirty physician graduates in my original sample reported highly problematic practices regarding miscarriage management as ethics committees in Catholic-owned hospitals, in order to avoid participating in abortion, prevented medical intervention until fetal death. In these cases, physicians delayed care, disobeyed or ignored committees (and risked their jobs), or transported patients to non-Catholic hospitals for treatment, sometimes requiring long ambulance rides and risks to patient safety. Catholic doctrine significantly limited physician autonomy, in some cases compromising the quality and safety of reproductive health care. Legally protected by institutionally applied "conscience clauses," such medicine is practiced according to the ideology of the health-care "managers" as opposed to the ideology of physicians or patients.

Through the course of my research, I spoke with a handful of abortion training faculty and administrators who, like Dr. Chasey, bemoaned how few of their residents went on to offer abortions to their patients after they graduated from their residency programs. Some took comfort in the fact that resident abortion training had helped to destigmatize abortion one doctor at a time. Their graduates would be more likely to empathize with patients seeking abortion and be able to explain exactly what to expect from the procedure. They would also be more competent in intrauterine surgical procedures generally. Those graduates trained in second-trimester abortion would be better at performing emergency uterine evacuation for late miscarriage or fetal demise. They may possibly continue performing abortions for less contested reasons (genetic and medical indications). At the minimum, their graduates would know how to make informed referrals to abortion clinics and provide better follow-up care. But in the end, most of the trainers and many of the trained were still disappointed in the realities of abortion care in the United States.

Autonomy Lost

Perhaps abortion rights activists who advocate the integration of abortion into mainstream medicine are basing their hopes on a nearly extinct model of health care. Despite the unique political turmoil surrounding abortion, many of the challenges to integration are linked to the loss in autonomy with which all physicians contend today. I have witnessed this firsthand. My father, husband, and sister-in-law are all family practice doctors who have worked with underserved populations for most of their careers. Through their eyes, I have seen two very different understandings of what it is to be a physician. My father was educated during the height of medicine's "golden age" in the 1960s, practiced in the 1970s, and experienced his "dethroning" vividly in the 1980s as managed care came to the fore. For the final two decades of his career he worked in a variety of medical settings and was often frustrated by various conditions of his work: how many patients his employers mandated that he see per hour, how little flexibility he had in his treatments and referrals, and fundamentally, how certain decisions were no longer under his purview. In stark contrast, my husband and sister-in-law never expected anything different. They were educated in the late 1990s, after "the fall"; they knew they would be employees who would have to work within a variety of complex organizational constraints.

The ob-gyn physicians I interviewed had similarly lowered expectations of their professional autonomy. As ob-gyns, they enjoy both higher prestige and higher pay than family practitioners; nevertheless, they have been subject to the same redistribution of medical power into the hands of employers, insurers, and even patients (Hafferty and Light 1995). Sociologists who study the professions have debated what these power shifts have meant for the status of the profession of medicine overall. For decades, some have theorized that the corporatization of medicine would so severely cripple physician autonomy that it would diminish the quality of health care and weaken American medicine (McKinlay and Marceau 2002; McKinlay and Stoeckle 1988). Others saw the rise of patients' rights and consumer health movements as a movement toward the "deprofessionalization" of physicians (Haug and Lavin 1978; Haug 1976; Haug 1988), eroding patient confidence and resulting in a population more inclined to use physicians as expert consultants rather than as authorities over their medical behavior, again decreasing the status of the profession. Sociological interest in the welfare of the medical profession has at times justified itself through evidence that physicians do a better job for patients when they are satisfied with their work (Linn et al. 1985). Physicians have been found to be more satisfied when they feel patients respect them, when they have control over nonphysicians working under them, and when they feel they are paid adequately (Warren, Weitz, and Kulis 1998). In other words, like most people, especially those accustomed to a certain amount of power, physicians are more satisfied when they feel they have more authority and are highly valued for their work.

Interestingly, in his later work Elliot Freidson (1984; 1994) argued that sociologists have been misguided for thinking that the status of the medical profession is declining, because, at the end of the day, physicians still control the content of their work, and their work is still highly esteemed. While he recognized that physician autonomy and authority are threatened by shifts in the financial structure of medicine, he argued that physicians are still at the top of the medical hierarchy, and hence they maintain high status as the keepers of complex knowledge not accessible to nonphysicians. Paradoxically, after inspiring decades of sociological inquiries aimed at critiquing physician abuses of power (Bosk 2006; Conrad 2006; Freidson 1970), Freidson argued the merits of physician (occupational) control of medicine, asserting that occupational control of health care is preferable to the alternatives of market or bureaucratic control (1984; 1994).

This debate over the decline of physician autonomy and how it has affected the medical profession is important to the specific context of obstetrics and gynecology. Just as ob-gyns learn during residency to assimilate legal concerns into their management of childbirth, they learn to expect that their medical judgment is not the only, nor necessarily the most important, factor in their decision making.[1] The physicians I interviewed are accustomed to the social and financial realms intruding on their medicine to a much greater degree than Americans are likely aware of. From the moment they graduate residency, most ob-gyns expect to become employees who work within the constraints of a private-practice group or a larger managing entity rather than as sovereign professionals. Once they become employees or partners, they quickly learn that abortion is not an acceptable practice in many mainstream medical settings, regardless of its high frequency and safety, their own technical proficiency, and their personal feelings about the morality of abortion. Thus my findings add complexity to Freidson's assertion (1984; 1994) that physicians still control the content of their work. As individual practitioners, in the case of abortion, they do not. If the medical profession were not deeply ambivalent about abortion (Joffe 1995), perhaps collectively physicians could effectively control the terms of abortion practice. But, in fact, the medical profession wavers in its support, the government impinges on its practice, the market pressures physicians to avoid it, and, thus, individual physicians outside of academia generally lack institutional protections necessary to incorporate abortion care into their work.

Systemic Constraints

By not actively fighting the constraints that limit their involvement with abortion and relegate its practice to the periphery of medicine, physicians and their organizations perpetuate the marginalization of abortion services. At the same time, the existing structure of services makes the inclusion of abortion in mainstream medical practice both impractical and professionally disadvantageous because of the threat of lost income, prestige, or both. In a vicious cycle, the professional marginalization of abortion care both creates and is created by the stigma and controversy around abortion. Physicians who want to offer abortion to their patients find they generally have just one (figurative) place to work: abortion clinics. The result is that providing abortions can mean giving up practicing the bulk of what they are trained to do. Most physicians in this study who were pro-choice and feeling quite bad about not providing abortion would not choose the "subspecialty" of abortion provider. When being an abortion provider means giving up creditability as a generalist, which is what they fear, only the most politically motivated doctors are left to the task.

Morality and Moral Authority in Abortion Care

If providing abortion is so professionally destructive, who wants to do it and why? The answer is, of course, primarily those who feel strongly that it is the right thing to do; those for whom it is a professional obligation of great proportion; and those who give abortion provision priority over other things in their lives (including personal safety, geographic location, professional prestige, and practice options). Physicians who make abortion much of their life's work believe it is a highly moral activity for a variety of reasons. Some physicians feel they are giving women their lives back, giving them a second chance. Some feel providing abortions protects women's human rights, that only a woman and not her government should regulate her reproduction. And some physicians focus on the public health benefits of legal, safe, and accessible abortion; they see their work as directly preventing maternal deaths, because history has shown that women tend to seek out abortion regardless of its legality. Many providers will reference all of these reasons and others to explain their commitment to abortion work.

A physician's moral authority in this context means something different from what it meant during American medicine's ascending years. During the early and mid-twentieth century, paternalism was unproblematic in the physician–patient relationship. Physicians' newfound possession of scientific expertise translated into an expectation that they knew how to use it. Patients and society, in general, expected physicians to know a great deal about right and wrong in matters of the body and sexual behavior. This moral authority granted physicians the power to define what was normal and appropriate for women's reproductive lives in particular and for their gender more broadly. Therefore, when a physician sympathized with a woman's desire for abortion and found it justifiable, that physician was trusted to know what was good and moral.

Legalization of abortion and a patients' rights movement, however, coincided in the 1970s, altering the dynamic between physicians and patients. Since *Roe v. Wade*, a woman can decide for herself when abortion is morally appropriate. The authority of the pregnant woman, as opposed to that of the physician, is paramount. This change in dynamics has undoubtedly (albeit unconsciously) diminished some physicians' interest in abortion care. With doctors now serving more as technicians than as moral arbiters, some doctors may see the problematic terrain of abortion as less appealing.

Since *Roe*, both morality and authority take on different dimensions in abortion care. Some physicians feel tremendous righteousness in being an abortion provider; that is, some physicians feel that trusting a woman to know when an abortion is right for her, and honoring that decision by performing the abortion for any reason (often not asking the reason), is a highly virtuous, moral activity. Other physicians who firmly refuse to end fetal life under any circumstances also claim a moral high ground. Regardless of the moral stance of physicians, however, they no longer hold the power to justify which abortions are performed. While many patients are undoubtedly influenced by physicians who make their opposition to abortion known to them, in practice women have the legal right and ability to refer themselves to abortion clinics. Symbolically, then, the heroic physician who "rescued" women from midwife abortions during criminalization in the late nineteenth century and "back-alley butchers" during legalization in the 1970s was no longer quite as heroic after *Roe*. Adding the numerous barriers to provision to the decreased physician heroism, even doctors who find abortion care morally righteous have relinquished the turf. Ultimately, fitting with the new economics of medicine, abortion served as a model for subspecialty care that could be readily contracted out.

Physicians who do provide abortion have found a new narrative in which to locate their power (they don't judge; they save women by ensuring their reproductive options), but it is incompatible with the mainstream narrative of medical power (advise, decipher, discriminate the right and wrong in patients' lives), and they are professionally devalued. While in my experience abortion providers do not lack a sense of the morality of their work, they fail to persuade others of this new locus of moral "authority." Ultimately, many must content themselves with the gratitude of patients over the esteem of their colleagues in mainstream medicine.

Million-Plus Abortions

Fortunately for women seeking abortions, there are physicians willing to prioritize their moral and professional commitments to abortion care. Although the abortion rate has declined somewhat, more than a million abortions are still performed in the United States every year. Most of these occur in freestanding abortion clinics like Planned Parenthood around the country. The physicians I interviewed—in conservative and liberal areas alike—regularly mentioned sending their patients to local abortion clinics for care. Sometimes by "local," they meant the only abortion clinic in their state. Planned Parenthood is often the only clinic able to survive in the most politically hostile communities because of the organization's national philanthropic resources. Doctors working in these clinics are in a sense subspecialists, doing abortion and contraceptive management as a large part, if not all, of their work.

Some physicians have chosen to embrace the fact that primarily social (rather than medical) requirements have created the subspecialty of abortion practice and make it official by doing a fellowship. The Fellowship in Family Planning has grown in popularity in recent years, so much so that soon it may be eligible for a subspecialty accreditation (Landy 2005).[2]

These fellows typically direct the abortion services in the residency program of their departments during their tenure while working and teaching in the abortion clinic and conducting research. The fellowship training encompasses some of the complex social and psychological aspects of care during pregnancy termination with attention to how reproductive politics affect the patient and resident experiences with abortion. Fellows graduate as rare experts in medically challenging and late-term abortions as well as contraceptive management. These fellowships help to lend status to abortion expertise and can destigmatize abortion practice in some settings. Many fellows graduate and then join other academic departments to continue to train residents and conduct research. But fellows who leave academics can experience the same constraints as other ob-gyns in the outside world, evidenced by Dr. Vivian Costa (see Chapter 3), who took a position in a large HMO that ultimately contracted out its abortion care.

An exception to the tendency for physicians to specialize almost exclusively in abortion is the arrangement commonly found in academic medical settings. Ob-gyn departments in universities often allow faculty members the option of teaching residents in the abortion clinic along with all of their other responsibilities. This means that a faculty member may have one or two days of abortion clinic duty a month while continuing to do other surgeries, deliveries, and clinics as well. It is likely that academic institutions have had more success integrating and sustaining abortion practice because physicians in academia are frequently more politically liberal than those outside education.

Another medical realm of integrated abortion practice can be found among specialists of perinatology or maternal–fetal medicine—two names for high-risk obstetrics. Some such physicians terminate pregnancies in private practice. During my interviews I heard about them doing abortions for only wanted, problem pregnancies (often by labor induction), either when the pregnancy compromised the patient's health or the fetus had genetic problems. Perinatologists and maternal–fetal medicine physicians appear to operate in the higher stratum of morally stratified and classed abortion care. Because wanted, problem pregnancies are often seen as the most "legitimate" types for termination in the medical community, patients with expansive insurance or more money can elect to have the specialist terminate their wanted pregnancies in a hospital rather than in an abortion clinic. However, such private-practice abortions make up a very small portion of yearly abortion procedures.

Ultimately, the political commitment of physicians working in dedicated abortion clinics by necessity compensates for the lack of mainstream inclusion of abortion care. I find this both inspirational and tragic: inspirational because there are so many individuals willing to make substantial professional and personal sacrifices to do what they believe is right; and tragic because their competence in meeting abortion needs is used to justify the continued marginalization of abortion care and does not require mainstream medicine to account for its failings. But what choice do these committed physicians have?

The Future of Abortion Care in the United States

This book has been unabashedly American-centric. I did not undertake the study of abortion care in any other country. If I had, I probably would have found that women are better served here than in most of the world (Grimes et al. 2006; Fawcus 2008). In the United States women are not (usually) risking life and limb to get an abortion, nor is it acceptable in most U.S. health-care settings to be overtly judgmental or hostile toward women seeking abortion services as it is in some countries (Harries, Stinson, and Orner 2009; Klingberg-Allvin et al. 2006; Warenius et al. 2006). Things could certainly be worse for women seeking abortion, and they are in many places; however, I did not select other places for comparison. Rather, my conceptual basis for comparison with abortion care in the United States was other kinds of health care in the United States. I asked, how is abortion different? How has it failed, despite the efforts of many committed advocates, to be "normal" health care? And though this is not an international study, it is nonetheless worth noting that the countries that treat abortion care relatively more like other medical procedures in a relatively less stigmatized fashion are largely found in Scandinavia, where socialized medicine has a stronger hold and ideological opposition to abortion a weaker one (Hammarstedt, Lalos, and Wulff 2006).

Alas, medicine is a business in the United States and not a universal entitlement of citizens as it is in such countries (although as this book goes to press the Obama administration has made a great stride toward changing this state of affairs). Thus, our health-care system is particularly vulnerable to social pressures and market forces. Since the "golden age" of medicine, those with power in health care are often nonclinician executives (or in the case of Catholic-owned health care, they are bishops, priests, and nuns) who want to limit involvement with abortion. Physician associations, although periodically vocal in defense of their right to control the technical and educational aspects of abortion care, have done relatively little to support a professional mandate or obligation to provide it. A revamping of American medicine in the form of a universal health-care system could have a major effect on reproductive medicine for better or for worse. If such a system were to sanction abortion by allocating resources to training and provision, its integration and normalization might increase. Given the widespread resistance to public funding for abortion, however, this scenario seems unlikely. It is more probable that abortion would be excluded from national health care, as it was in the Obama administration's 2010 health insurance reform law, and abortion services would be even less supported and integrated than they are today.

In light of the structural barriers facing physicians who want to perform abortions within mainstream medical practices, abortion rights advocates may want to target a different population of physicians to create a new provider base. Advocacy groups have sensibly focused on politicizing physicians early in their careers, but new doctors like those in my study perceive themselves as financially and professionally vulnerable. Therefore, advocacy groups may want to emphasize targeting doctors later in their careers by offering them opportunities for training or retraining in abortion care. Doctors in their fifties offer several advantages in addressing the problems of abortion care. First, they are well established in their careers and may be more successful in taking the risk of incorporating abortion into their practices. Second, some relatively senior physicians may want to retire from their call schedules, especially ob-gyns and family practice physicians who do obstetrics. After decades of working nights, such physicians might welcome the opportunity to give up doing deliveries and have more daytime income opportunities. Third, if their children are grown, older physicians may feel relatively less concern for their families' safety and financial security given those risks of abortion practice. And, fourth, some physicians may want an opportunity to do political work, perhaps a few days a month in an abortion clinic, but they may be unsure how to start so late in their careers. A friendly and accessible abortion clinic could provide time for observation and training to get them up to speed.

I am not arguing that activists should give up on new physicians or that doctors approaching retirement could or should be responsible for completely alleviating the shortages of abortion providers. Of course, the involvement of new physicians in abortion care is imperative, and new physicians appear to be entering the field, evidenced by the fact that the rate of decline in providers has slowed significantly since 2000. Given that the barriers to integrated abortion practice do not appear to be lessening (although this is difficult to measure) and that many of the older abortion providers have been retiring, the slowing in the decline of abortion providers indicates that more new physicians may be subspecializing (formally or informally) in abortion care. Improvements in abortion training since the mid-1990s may be responsible for this. The tremendous effect of the 1996 ACGME mandate to train ob-gyn residents in abortion (regardless of Congress's attempt to make it unenforceable) indicates that institutions can rapidly change their practices when their organizations sanction a marginalized activity. Yet even in this rare instance in which the medical profession rallied to support abortion, the effect of the ACGME mandate would not likely have been as great without the addition of pro-choice philanthropy. A significant amount of improvement in abortion training can be credited to the Kenneth J. Ryan Residency Training Program in Abortion and Family Planning, which has grown tremendously during the past decade, providing funding and curriculums to forty-two ob-gyn residency programs in the United States and one in Canada.[3] The question remains, how can abortion *practice* gain the same legitimacy that has been gained for abortion *training*?

Ironically, access to abortion care could ultimately be saved by nonphysicians, and by this I do not mean activists and philanthropists, but rather nonphysician abortion providers. A century after the medical profession claimed abortion as its own from competing practitioners, it might indeed give it back. Although the medical profession has been notoriously turf hungry vis-à-vis nurse practitioners, physician assistants, and certified nurse midwives (collectively called advanced practice clinicians [APCs]), abortion may be a case in which physicians yield the territory

(Weitz, Anderson, and Taylor 2009). APCs currently provide medication abortions under physician supervision in many states. They have also attained limited rights to perform first-trimester aspiration abortions in a few states, the safety of which has been demonstrated in some settings.[4] Recently in California, the Access through Primary Care Initiative embarked on an experimental training program to demonstrate that APCs trained in abortion care have a high safety record so that they can legally begin to fill gaps left by physicians in abortion care. If this effort is successful and inspires similar programs in other states, APCs may offer the most promise for abortion access, given the effects of abortion politics on physician practice.

Indeed, pro-choice activists, philanthropists, and even academicians have worked in several ways to compensate for shortcomings in the medical practice of abortion. The next step for these actors will be to find a way to successfully pressure medical professional associations, health networks, hospitals, and private-practice groups to challenge prohibitions on abortion care—or at least to stop tolerating them and thereby helping them to proliferate. Public health–minded HMOs and physician practices could significantly change the world of abortion care if they stopped outsourcing it. Perhaps by bringing attention to the widespread buck-passing of abortion care on all of these fronts, some of these medical organizations may stop accepting the segregation of abortion from mainstream medicine as a matter of course and be forced to account for the practice.

Ultimately, by looking beyond stories of physician bravery or lack thereof to find answers to what ails abortion care in the United States, I found widespread constraints on physicians' abilities to provide abortion. These structural forces explain why abortion providers have been declining in number even after significant improvements in physician training. In the end, American medical professional associations must use their power to legitimize abortion within medicine in order to effectively counter the institutionalized buck-passing of abortion care. Concurrently, advocacy groups must, of course, continue their work. And neither should expect that physicians can change the forces impeding abortion practice by running on their political commitment alone. They may be *willing* to try, but as I have demonstrated here, they are not necessarily *able* to do it on their own.

Abortion Terminology

ASPIRATION: Suctioning out the contents of the uterus with a machine or manual vacuum technique. (Most first-trimester abortions are technically aspiration procedures, not surgical procedures, because surgery implies the cutting of tissue. However, the term "surgical" was more commonly used to refer to such procedures by participants in the study and is more readily understood by readers. Therefore, I chose to refer to aspirations as surgical procedures in many places throughout the book.)

D&C (DILATION AND CURETTAGE): Emptying the contents of the uterus by dilating the cervix and scraping the side walls of the uterus with a curved instrument to evacuate all tissue. For pregnancies of not more than thirteen weeks. Most of the procedure is currently done with an aspiration/suction device. Procedure duration: Five to fifteen minutes.

D&E (DILATION AND EVACUATION): Same as a D&C with the addition of surgically removing the larger fetus. Typically done in women who are aborting or miscarrying when between thirteen and twenty-four weeks' gestation. Procedure duration: Usually fifteen to thirty minutes.

D&X (DILATION AND EXTRACTION): Also known as a *partial-birth abortion* (see below). Similar to the D&E in duration time and gestational period, but the fetus is removed intact. The procedure was rarely done before it was banned for political reasons.

ELECTIVE ABORTION: An abortion that is done for reasons other than genetic or medical reasons, such as reasons related to poverty, career, mental health, separation/divorce, drugs, etc. Technically, genetically indicated terminations are also elected by the pregnant woman, but they are usually perceived as more "legitimate" and therefore are grouped with medical rather than social reasons for termination. *Note*: One abortion clinic I am aware of separated abortions by *maternal indications* (includes all elective reasons) and *fetal indications* (includes all medical and genetic reasons).

GENETICALLY INDICATED ABORTION: (1) *Fetal anomaly*—the fetus is not developing "normally" and is likely to be born unhealthy or with a disability of some sort; (2) *fatal fetal anomaly*—something is wrong with the fetus that makes life impossible outside the uterus.

INDUCTION OF LABOR: An abortion that is done without surgical instruments, but rather with medications that induce labor so the woman's uterus expels the pregnancy. Usually takes place in a hospital labor and delivery ward. For women aborting, miscarrying, or experiencing fetal demise in the second or third trimester of pregnancy. Procedure duration: Usually less than twenty-four hours. Other terms: *induction, labor induction, KCl injection*.

MEDICALLY INDICATED ABORTION: An abortion that is done when the pregnancy is hazardous to the pregnant woman's health or life.

MEDICATION ABORTION, MEDICAL ABORTION: An early abortion (typically fewer than nine weeks' gestation) induced usually with a combination of the drug mifepristone (the "French abortion pill," RU-486) or methotrexate (a drug used in the treatment of cancer) with misoprostol (which causes contractions and cervical softening). Misoprostol alone is less effective, but because of its affordability and over-the-counter status in Latin America, it has been studied and used widely. A medication abortion can be done at home, and the physical experience is similar to severe menstrual cramps. A woman may have just a few hours of cramping and bleeding, or days of bleeding and spotting, with intermittent episodes of severe cramping. The unpredictability of the side effects and duration is what causes many women to choose a surgical procedure.

PARTIAL-BIRTH ABORTION: A term made up solely for political reasons by antiabortion activists in order to ban an abortion during which the fetus is extracted intact (see *D&X*). The legal language of the final ruling of the Supreme Court (*Gonzales v. Carhart* 2007) was so vague as to make many practitioners and lawyers fear that it could apply to all second-trimester abortions.

SELECTIVE REDUCTION: Usually used in conjunction with fertility treatments that result in multiple embryos. The uterus is viewed by ultrasound, and an injection is made directly into the embryonic sac to kill one or more of the embryos, thus reducing the number carried to term.

A Methodological Note on City Size

I have replaced the names of cities where doctors work with three terms related to city size. There is no consistent demographic terminology that correlates to these three sizes. According to the U.S. Census Bureau's definitions, all three are considered "metropolitan statistical areas." Therefore, I made these divisions with the sensitizing perspective of the physicians themselves.

A city with a population of less than 100,000 is often described by physicians as a *small town* in my study because they perceive themselves as both a scarce resource and a visible pseudo-public figure where they live. Physicians similarly described certain *midsized cities*. This tended to be the case if the city was relatively isolated—that is, not near other large cities or medical training hubs, and not the core of a large population. *Urban areas* tended to offer physicians relatively more anonymity, academic institutional support, and plentiful referral options for abortion care.

In summary:

URBAN AREA: A statistical area as demarcated by the Census Bureau (large cities, smaller ones, and suburbs in proximity) that has a population size greater than 500,000.

MIDSIZED CITY: A city with a population of 100,000–500,000 and not within one hour's commute of a large city; that is, it is isolated from other sizable cities and suburbs.

SMALL TOWN: A city whose population is less than 100,000 (with rural inhabitants bringing the area up to 150,000 or fewer) and isolated; that is, it is not a suburb of a larger city or metropolitan area. It is likely the center for some rural areas.

The table shows how the practices of the thirty physicians interviewed for this study were distributed in this scheme of city size at the time they were interviewed.

Locations by City Size
of Physicians' Practices at Time of Interview

	URBAN AREA	MIDSIZED CITY	SMALL TOWN	TOTAL
Male	4	1	3	8
Female	15	5	2	22
TOTAL	19	6	5	30

NOTES

Notes to Chapter 1

1. All names of individuals interviewed for this book are pseudonyms in order to protect the confidentiality of the study participants.

2. On January 22, 1973, the Supreme Court legalized abortion with its decision in *Roe v. Wade.* Women thereafter had the right to terminate a pregnancy up to the gestational point of viability (when a fetus can survive outside the womb with medical assistance), which was considered to be about twenty-eight weeks' gestation at the time of the decision, but with medical advances is currently closer to twenty-four weeks. (For an accessible overview about medical understandings of fetal viability see Krissi Danielsson, "Premature Birth and Viability," About.com, *miscarriage.about.com/od/pregnancyafterloss/a/prematurebirth.htm.*) In the *Roe* decision, abortion rights during the first trimester of pregnancy were granted nationally, although some states had already begun to change their laws. An online resource for Supreme Court cases summarized the case thus: "The Court held that a woman's right to an abortion fell within the right to privacy (recognized in *Griswold v. Connecticut*) protected by the Fourteenth Amendment. The decision gave a woman total autonomy over the pregnancy during the first trimester and defined different levels of state interest for the second and third trimesters. As a result, the laws of 46 states were affected by the Court's ruling" (Oyez, U.S. Supreme Court Media, *www.oyez.org/cases/1970-1979/1971/1971_70_18/*).

3. An *elective abortion* stands in contrast to an abortion that is done for medical reasons—because the fetus is not healthy or the woman's health is endangered by the pregnancy. Physicians I spoke with differentiated these two groups of abortions regularly, and elective abortions are often perceived as more political and less legitimate than those they refer to as "genetic" or "maternal health" terminations. These distinctions are socially constructed, of course. A woman may elect to terminate or not terminate any pregnancy, whether she or the fetus is healthy or not. And women who are raped or experiencing severe poverty or abuse may feel they have no choice but to "elect" abortion. However, for the

purposes of communicating the concepts of abortion known to physicians, elective abortions here specifically refer to those procedures without a medical diagnosis of maternal or fetal health problems.

Perhaps because of abortion stigma and the desire of many people *not* to say the word *abortion*, there are many different terms and abbreviations commonly used instead of *abortion*, even when such differentiation is not medically necessary: evacuation of the uterus, or uterine evacuation; termination, or pregnancy termination; AB (abortion); TAB (therapeutic abortion); VIP (voluntary interruption of pregnancy); TOP (termination of pregnancy); and missed AB (miscarriage). See also Appendix A.

4. This is based on a comparison of data available on the incidence of medical procedures nationally. Owings and Kozak (1998) provide the most recent presentation of all hospital and ambulatory procedures together but eliminate abortion clinics from their data sources. They reported that for women of reproductive age in 1996 the most common procedures were birth related; number one was episiotomy, at 1.29 million. In 1996, abortion was the most common procedure, at 1.36 million. In the 2005 National Hospital Discharge Survey, DeFrances and Hall (2007) showed that the number of episiotomies had gone down dramatically to 537,000, but cesarean sections had risen to 1.29 million. For comparison, Jones et al. (2008) showed that abortion declined to 1.21 million in 2005. Therefore, in 2005 the abortion rate dipped below the caesarean section rate. Jones et al. (2008) attribute the abortion decline to increased contraceptive use, lower unintended pregnancy, more women carrying unintended pregnancies to term, and decreased access to abortions in certain geographical areas.

5. Laura Nader coined the expression *studying up* in her analysis of power dynamics between the researcher and the researched. She challenged social scientists to find out more about the social world of the powerful, despite the fact that they are able to insulate themselves from outside examination more easily than groups with less power.

6. When using the term *pro-choice* in regard to a person, I specifically mean someone who supports the legal right of a woman to have an abortion if she chooses. I often use the term *abortion rights advocate* or *activist* to signify people who devote significant energy toward ensuring reproductive rights, access, and quality of care, beyond the basic pro-choice commitment to legality. When I use pro-choice in regard to an organization or movement, there is an additional acknowledgment of affiliation with that side of the hyperpartisan abortion wars.

7. Although *Roe v. Wade* grants women abortion rights under the authority of the physician, in a few states advanced practice clinicians (nurse practitioners, physician assistants, and midwives) are making inroads into this medical territory by providing mostly medication and sometimes surgical (or aspiration) abortion procedures. See Abortion Access Project, "Advanced Practice Clinicians," *www.abortionaccess.org/content/view/37/88/*, accessed November 9, 2009.

8. One of the earliest medical sociologists, Talcott Parsons, likened the role of the physician within the family to that of clergy because of the tendency for physicians to be present during end-of-life and other pivotal moments. Indeed Parsons's characterization as such is fitting with the increased secularization of Americans in the twentieth century. Americans, by and large, became less oriented toward God and more oriented toward health as a higher calling. Physicians, as the gatekeepers of health information, were thus highly revered.

9. The early abortion history provided in this chapter relies predominantly on the work of James C. Mohr (1978), Kristin Luker (1984), and Leslie Reagan (1997) unless cited otherwise.

10. In 1992, in his work on medical ethics and the medical profession, sociologist Robert Zussman argued that the medical ethics movement that proliferated since the mid-1960s (it was strongest perhaps from the 1970s to the 1990s) was precisely a project in dismantling the power of physicians. Zussman attributed the movement's success to the "waning of medicine's cultural authority." He provided the following three explanations for this trend: trust in experts in general had declined since the 1960s; a new "sense of boundless financing" and entitlement to health care following the advent of Medicare and Medicaid in 1965 brought escalating medical costs and resulted in external bodies ("big business and big government") managing care after the 1980s; and finally, increased specialization within medicine eroded the personal ties between primary care physicians and their patients (Zussman 1992: 6–7).

11. Statistics are drawn from the American Medical Association's report "Physician Characteristics and Distribution in the US, 2008 Edition" and are presented in tables 1, 5, and 15 on the AMA web page "Women Physician's Congress: Statistics and History," *www.ama-assn.org/ama/pub/about-ama/our-people/member-groups-sections/women-physicians-congress/statistics-history.shtml.*

Notes to Chapter 2

1. In 1970, Dr. Hodgson intentionally performed an illegal abortion while practicing in her home state, Minnesota. It was a well-publicized attempt to compel legal change around abortion, although ultimately *Roe* beat her to the punch, as *Roe v. Wade* was tried first in the Supreme Court and overruled Hodgson's conviction in Minnesota. While awaiting trial in Minnesota, she had worked in Washington, D.C., where abortion was already legalized, as the medical director of Preterm, one of the first large freestanding abortion clinics in the country. Carole Joffe's *Doctors of Conscience* (1995) gives a detailed account of Hodgson's story. Hodgson remained outspoken on abortion rights until her death in 2006.

2. For example, the Primary Care Initiative is a project designed to assess the safety of teaching advanced practice clinicians to perform aspiration abortion proce-

dures. See ANSIRH, Advancing New Standards in Reproductive Health, "Primary Care Initiative," *www.ansirh.org/research/pci.php.*

3. The CDC did not collect data from California, so estimates are low. The number of abortions peaked in 1990 at 1.61 million and declined slowly until 2005 (the most recent data) to 1.21 million (Jones et al. 2008).

4. The APHA and ACOG overtly supported creating accessible, safe, and legal abortion services. In 1968 the APHA had called for an all-out repeal of abortion laws, and after the *Roe* decision ACOG issued a statement "urging that first trimester abortions be performed either in hospitals or in licensed clinics with hospital back-up services" (Joffe 1995: 50). The latter would become the prevailing model of the post-*Roe* era.

5. Joffe writes, "The AMA's only major statement on abortion in this period was a resolution adopted by its House of Delegates in June 1973 stipulating that abortions be performed only by licensed physicians in accredited hospitals" and that "physicians with conscientious objections to abortion be free to withdraw from these cases" (Joffe 1995: 49).

6. Cases brought against Margaret Sanger for distributing contraceptives in the early twentieth century were won by granting such authority to physicians. Most significantly, however, *Griswold v. Connecticut* in 1965 legalized contraception based on a constitutional right to privacy. The penumbra of privacy was extended in the *Roe* decision to the physician–patient relationship (Rose 2007: 64–65).

7. The violence and disruption statistics of the National Abortion Federation are regularly updated. See "Violence Statistics," *www.prochoice.org/about_abortion /violence/violence_statistics.html*, accessed November 10, 2009.

8. For information about FACE see U.S. Department of Justice, Civil Rights Division, "Freedom of Access to Clinics Entrances (FACE) Act," *www.usdoj.gov/crt /split/facestat.htm,* and National Abortion Federation, "Freedom of Access to Clinic Entrances (FACE) Act," *www.prochoice.org/about_abortion/facts/face_act .html,* both accessed November 10, 2009.

9. For updated details on state policies, see the National Abortion Federation, "U.S. Public Policy," *www.prochoice.org/policy/states/states_threats.html*, and the Guttmacher Institute, "State Policies in Brief," *www.guttmacher.org/statecenter /spibs/spib_OAL.pdf,* both accessed November 10, 2009.

10. Medical Students for Choice "work to make reproductive health care, including abortion, a part of standard medical education and residency training" (from the group's mission statement, at *medicalstudentsforchoice.org/index .php?page=about-us*). Physicians for Reproductive Choice and Health "works with medical and women's health organizations that share an interest in expanding and improving the medical options and quality of services available to American women and their families" (from "About: Our Mission," *www.prch .org/about-our-mission*). Also see the Abortion Access Project mission state-

ment, at *www.abortionaccess.org/content/view/15/89/*, which states that the group "seeks to catalyze changes within health care and reproductive health activism that increase the participation of a wide range of health care providers in providing and connecting women to safe abortion care." All accessed November 23, 2009.

11. Studies from the mid-1980s show that while solo practices were already becoming less common, three-quarters of nonfederal physicians remained self-employed (meaning they owned part or all of their medical practices) (Kletke et al. 1996; Marder et al. 1988). Twenty years later, no longer in business for themselves, physicians have largely become employees of health-care organizations or large group practices. By 2005, only 15 percent of physicians were self-employed. The rest were wage and salary employees of physician group practices (50 percent), hospitals (18 percent), and governmental, academic, or other health clinic employers (17 percent). (The latter statistics are from Bureau of Labor Statistics, *Occupational Outlook Handbook, 2008–09 Edition,* "Physicians and Surgeons, Employment," *www.bls.gov/oco/ocos074.htm#emply*, accessed September 5, 2009.) However, it is very difficult to gauge these trends precisely over time. Measurements have been inconsistent and the above sources may have "compared apples and oranges." Health policy researchers of physician employment changes write, "Despite their potential importance, relatively little is known about medical groups, perhaps because they are more difficult to study than health insurance plans or hospitals" (Casalino et al. 2003: 1958). Statistics from the Community Tracking Study of the Center for Studying Health System Change are showing less stark declines in physician practice ownership than those indicated by the comparison of 1980s and 1990s data and the recent data from the Bureau of Labor Statistics (above), but they demonstrate similar trends away from small group physician ownership (Casalino et al. 2003; Liebhaber and Grossman 2007).

12. The medical term *D&X* refers to an abortion when the fetus comes out intact (as opposed to dismembered). Many agreed that the construction of the case was ludicrous because the method deemed as a "partial birth" is rarely used and not particularly more or less "humane" than its alternative. One ob-gyn I interviewed remarked: "It's just comical to me that it's a political term . . . If you ask any doctors what's a partial-birth abortion, nobody really has an answer as to what that means." And a perinatologist told me: "I still really can't figure out exactly what a partial-birth abortion is . . . So, if they want to ban it, fine, because I don't think it really even exists." However, the naming and banning of a surgical technique for abortion turned out to be a successful tactic by pro-life activists as they managed to involve government in abortion regulation at a higher level and get the whole country talking about fetal pain, fetal dismemberment, and fetal rights.

13. This observation comes from Tracy Weitz (personal communication), who witnessed and has written about these proceedings (Weitz and Yanow 2008).

14. News Release, "HHS Secretary Calls on Certification Group to Protect Conscience Rights," March 14, 2008, *www.hhs.gov/news/press/2008pres/03/20080314a.html*, accessed November 23, 2009.

15. *Medication abortion*—also called *medical abortion, the (French) abortion pill*, or *RU-486*—generally refers to the drug mifepristone, which became legal in the United States in 2000, twelve years after it was made available in Europe. Mifepristone blocks the hormone progesterone, which is necessary to the development of the pregnancy. The drug is usually combined with misoprostol to expel the pregnancy tissue and lining (misoprostol is an ulcer medication that causes uterine contractions and is widely used off-label to facilitate labor and delivery). See National Abortion Federation, Abortion Facts, "What Is Medical Abortion?," *www.prochoice.org/about_abortion/facts/medical_abortion.html*, accessed November 10, 2009. Medication abortion actually refers to any medication that causes abortion. Misoprostol as well as the cancer drug methotrexate can be used to terminate pregnancy in the absence of mifepristone, but they are not quite as effective and can have more unpleasant side effects. However, in low-resource countries, especially in Latin America, where misoprostol is widely available at pharmacies, women frequently use misoprostol to self-induce abortion, and its availability is believed to have reduced abortion-related deaths around the world (Fernandez et al. 2009; Harper et al. 2007). Medication abortion is not the same thing as the "morning-after pill," also called *emergency contraception*, which is a strong dose of birth control medication and can prevent the implantation of a pregnancy if taken within a few days of unprotected sex (emergency contraception cannot abort or damage an implanted pregnancy).

16. For an intimate and harrowing account of the abortion provider commuting experience, see Wicklund and Kesselheim 2007.

Notes to Chapter 3

1. This is much smaller than the 47 percent found in a survey of five California residency programs, which, because of their routine training and location, offered the least restrictive social conditions for abortion training (Steinauer et al. 2003).

2. Family practice and internal medicine doctors are increasingly interested in and able to perform abortions as more of their residencies have included elective (usually not routine) abortion training in recent years (Brahmi et al. 2007; Dehlendorf et al. 2007). As mentioned earlier, advanced practice clinicians (nurse practitioners, physician assistants, or midwives) are also beginning to find entrée into abortion provision. See Abortion Access Project, "Advanced Practice Clinicians," *www.abortionaccess.org/content/view/37/88/*, accessed November 23, 2009.

3. The human fertilized egg is called an embryo weeks two through eight after fertilization; after this point it is considered a fetus.

4. According to the National Abortion Federation's statistics on violence and disruption in clinics, nine of eleven murders and attempted murders of abortion providers were in urban/suburban areas (specifically, cities that were part of larger metropolitan areas with populations of more than five hundred thousand). Both exceptions took place in Pensacola, Florida. See National Abortion Federation, "History of Violence/Murders and Shootings," *www.prochoice.org/about_abortion/violence/murders.asp*, accessed November 23, 2009.

Notes to Chapter 4

1. I heard disparate stories from people in the same residency programs as to whether "partial participation" was required for opt-outs. It may have been strongly suggested, but not officially required. Furthermore, policies probably changed over time with different directors. Since my interviews were snapshots of experiences within a five-year range and relied on memories that were five to ten years old, the varying perceptions and recollections did not line up seamlessly.

2. I followed up with the question: "What are some other things that are uncomfortable in obstetrics and gynecology?" He answered: "There's really nothing that's as emotionally packed as abortion is. But that's a great question. What could you sort of rank up there as that unpleasant? Emotionally, nothing. I'm trying to think of a good way to describe it and the gist of what our professors were referring to. There's a lot of—the way babies come out—blood, poop, mucus, it's messy. It's the middle of the night. You have to take call. Usually stuff's happening at 3 o'clock in the morning. All those things are not necessarily pleasant—the 3 o'clock in the morning and getting puked on, pooped on, amniotic fluid everywhere—that kind of stuff. That's unpleasant. But you can't say: 'I don't want to do that. I'm not going to take call, I'm only going to deliver babies in the daytime and not the nighttime.' Or somebody has an infection and they come in for gynecologic purposes, and [it's] unpleasant because it smells or it's messy, but you can't [say] 'I'm not going to treat people that have smelly infections.' It's just not an option. It's not an option to opt out. So, I mean, that's part of it. But are there other areas of ob-gyn that are as emotionally entangled as abortion is? I don't think so. I don't think I can come up with another area that creates that kind of angst either with patients or with providers."

3. In Chapter 6, the relatively moderate nature of Dr. Gray's abortion views are demonstrated. Also, below she shares a story where she advocated for a patient with a fatal fetal anomaly and 2.5 months of pregnancy remaining. Dr. Gray was aware of the hardship on the woman and tried to expedite the delivery, but

she was unable to do so in her hospital or the other nearby hospitals because they are all Catholic owned or affiliated. She tried to get permission from her Catholic ethics committee to induce labor but was rejected: "I've got [a patient] now, the lady has a known fetal anomaly that's not compatible with life, and none of the hospitals locally will let us induce somebody that has a live baby inside. It's still an abortion, I mean, it is, it's an abortion, so they don't allow abortions at all . . . they will make an exception in the rare circumstance that it's going to affect the mom's life. But this one, you know, she's healthy. It's just the baby that's not going to live . . . They have an ethics committee that meets every month—and I had submitted the lady with the abnormal baby, and then they declined it, which I sort of knew they would. Now she's too far along. She was going to go to the abortion clinic, and that was the problem. She was too far along already at that point. The baby had a growth spurt, and they wouldn't do it. So the only option for her at that point was to go out of state. There were some places she could go, but it was too expensive, but they told her about someplace in Kansas . . . But she was going to have to fly to Kansas, and it was something like $6,000 and she didn't have the money, so . . . If the baby dies in utero, obviously they'd let us induce her at that point, but not as long as the baby's still alive. So yeah, at this point she's still looking like she's going to go to term." The clinic she refers to in Kansas was that of Dr. George Tiller, who was murdered by an antiabortion extremist in May 2009. Unfortunately, Dr. Gray did not realize that philanthropic funds were available for poor women to help defray costs. The clinic was closed after Dr. Tiller's death; however, a group of doctors in New Mexico collaborated less than a year later to fill this gap in care.

4. From Medline Plus: "The chorion is the portion of fetal membrane that eventually forms the fetal side of the placenta. The chorion contains chorionic villi, which are small finger-like projections"; *www.nlm.nih.gov/medlineplus/ency/imagepages/9181.htm*, accessed May 29, 2008.

5. *Scut work* is a term used to refer to low-prestige work, paperwork, and various preparatory or cleanup work, often repetitive in nature and believed to confer little training or learning benefit. A widely used term in medical training, "scut work" refers to low-glamour duties typically delegated to medical students and lower-level residents by those higher up (Hayward et al. 1991).

6. What follows is the deleted portion of the medically graphic story: "It was sort of like one of those audible bleeding situations with the blood on the floor and there was no time to even do an exam. We just ran her up to the operating room, literally, just running to the elevator . . . physically pushed people out of the way to get into an operating room because that's how much bleeding—Yelling at everybody, 'Put her to sleep, put her to sleep!' It was an ER trauma situation and the anesthesiologist put her to sleep . . . Everybody's screaming at me. And we get her legs up in stirrups and there's blood everywhere . . . And they're like,

'Hmm, her blood looks like water.' She had a hemoglobin of 3. You know, she was in florid DIC . . . Fortunately, we were able to save her uterus. I've learned some tricks from some of the older guys about doing an anterior and posterior colpotomy, kind of opening the abdomen from the vagina and then just putting big clamps on the uterine arteries. And so we did that and that stopped the bleeding pretty much right away, because if we'd opened her she probably would have had a hysterectomy. And then [we] let her sit in the ICU for three days with clamps hanging out of her vagina while everything clotted off. And then we took her back to the OR and took the clamps off and she wasn't bleeding anymore."

7. The term *septic* refers to *sepsis*, a dangerous medical condition of inflammation throughout the body caused by infection.

8. Smith and Kleinman (1989) and Leif and Fox (1963) discuss how medical students learn to detach from the humanity of their subjects or objects of learning, whether they are corpses to dissect or people to examine, as well as how they detach from their own emotional reactions. Parsons (1951) relates how physicians learn to display "affective neutrality" despite their personal beliefs as part of their work.

9. *Abrupting* signifies that the patient is experiencing a placental abruption, when the placenta starts to separate from the uterus, cutting off nutrition and threatening the health/life of the fetus. The "coke" she refers to is the drug cocaine, which can cause early abruption.

10. I add quotation marks to the term *evidence-based* because it is thrown around so casually within medicine to indicate the "best" medical practices based on existing research. The problem is that there is a lot of subjectivity as to how we evaluate what is best, and for whom. Scholars studying the social world of science, technology, and medicine know this well. Often the highest criterion when evaluating whether a practice is "evidence based" is patient safety, but organizational dynamics, comfort, patient acceptability, administrative considerations, and cost are often factored into such evaluations as well. Timmermans and Berg (2003) provide an in-depth inquiry into the social complexities of medical standards and evidence-based medicine.

11. *DIC* refers to disseminated intravascular coagulation, "a condition in which small blood clots develop throughout the bloodstream . . . The increased clotting depletes the platelets and clotting factors needed to control bleeding . . . The excessive clotting is usually stimulated by a substance that enters the blood as part of a disease (such as an infection or certain cancers) or as a complication of childbirth, retention of a dead fetus, or surgery . . . If the condition follows surgery or childbirth, bleeding may be uncontrollable." Merck Manuals, Online Medical Library, "Disseminated Intravascular Coagulation (DIC)," *www.merck .com/mmhe/sec14/ch173/ch173h.html*, accessed November 23, 2009.

12. Perinatal hospice is the extension of the hospice philosophy of caring for dying individuals during their last days and weeks of life (after medical interventions

have ceased) to the experience of pregnancy loss. The Perinatal Hospice website (*www.perinatalhospice.org*, accessed November 23, 2009) begins: "If you are here because of a prenatal diagnosis that indicates your baby likely will die before or after birth, we are so sorry. Perhaps you are considering continuing your pregnancy and embracing whatever time you may be able to have with your baby, even if that time is only before birth, while your baby is cradled safely inside of you. Please know that support is available (see the links on this site for perinatal hospices and other resources) and that you are not alone. Parents who have traveled this path before you have found that it can be a beautiful, profoundly meaningful, and healing journey."

13. Many states require that patients be read specific information (sometimes called *right-to-know legislation*) with the objective of persuading women not to follow through with the abortion. One pro-choice advocacy group summarizes the content of these information requirements as follows: "The information is designed to persuade women to carry their pregnancies to term, and it generally includes descriptions of fetal development, adoption programs, and state laws requiring fathers to pay child support" (see Center for Reproductive Rights, "Mandatory Delays and Biased Counseling for Women Seeking Abortions," *reproductive rights.org/en/project/mandatory-delays-and-biased-counseling-for-women -seeking-abortions*, accessed November 23, 2009). Dr. Anderson said about her experience with right-to-know information: "Basically, it's two pages of things you have to read verbatim, ridiculous things like, 'the father of the baby is liable' and 'child support can be given through the state' and things that are fine if it's an elective abortion. But for couples who have a fatal diagnosis—!'"

Notes to Chapter 5

Portions of this chapter appeared in Lori R. Freedman, Uta Landy, Philip Darney, and Jody Steinauer, "Obstacles to the integration of abortion in obstetrics and gynecology practice," *Perspectives on Sexual and Reproductive Health*, 2010.

1. The organization Medical Students for Choice has proliferated and become active in many medical schools, and private sources of funding have enabled residency programs to improve abortion training and the teaching curriculum, which includes a politicizing component.

2. Goffman, who wrote briefly about several types of deviants who resisted their prescribed stigma, might have grouped abortion providers among "social deviants." He writes: "those who come together into a sub-community or milieu may be called *social deviants*, and their corporate life a deviant community . . . prostitutes, gypsies, carnival workers, hobos, winos, show people" (Goffman 1963: 143). Abortion providers have their own conferences and national organizations to help protect physicians from harm and support their professional endeavors. Specialized organizations may be typical for particular subspecialties in medi-

cine, but not for particular surgical procedures. This is a distinction of social, not medical, significance.

3. Pharmacists have been very vocal in a national "right of refusal," or "conscience clause," movement that lobbies for the right for a variety of practitioners to refuse to provide any treatment or medication to which they object, including contraceptive pills, emergency contraception, and in this case, misoprostol.

4. Cytotec, known by the generic name misoprostol, is approved by the Food and Drug Administration for use with ulcers, but it is universally used off-label for obstetrical care, namely, to induce uterine contractions and soften the cervix during childbirth. It is also used to facilitate medication abortion, in which case it is typically paired with mifepristone (RU-486 or the "French abortion pill") or methotrexate, a common cancer drug that works similarly to mifepristone and is more readily accessible to physicians but that has more uncomfortable side effects. Antiabortion legislation has created prohibitive amounts of paperwork requirements for mifepristone (Joffe and Weitz 2003). Cytotec/misoprostol can, however, cause an abortion if used by itself in the right doses. It is commonly used for this purpose throughout the world, especially in many Latin American countries, where it is sold in pharmacies over the counter.

5. Pregnancy terminations for genetic indications do not differ medically or surgically from elective procedures in most cases, and abortion clinics routinely do abortions for both reasons. A maternal health problem might necessitate doing the abortion in a hospital rather than at an outpatient clinic.

6. Most definitive genetic testing can happen only in the second trimester, and therefore, most patients are not able to make the decision to terminate if they so choose until about sixteen to twenty weeks of pregnancy for genetic reasons.

7. In order to address concerns about medical safety and reduce resident errors caused by fatigue, in 2003 the ACGME mandated a limit of eighty hours on the resident workweek. These limits include the moonlighting hours sanctioned by the residency; that is, residents are not allowed to hit their maximum hours at the residency program and then work additional hours for the residency's hospital in order to make more money. The residency may not be able to officially prohibit moonlighting outside the program (such as in an abortion clinic), but it can strongly discourage it. See the ACGME policy, "Duty Hours Language," *www.acgme.org/acWebsite/dutyHours/dh_Lang703.pdf*.

Notes to Chapter 6

Portions of this chapter appeared in Lori R. Freedman, Uta Landy, and Jody Steinauer, "When there's a heartbeat: Miscarriage management in Catholic-owned hospitals," *American Journal of Public Health*, 2008.

1. Even Catholic patients may not know that certain procedures are banned by Catholic hospitals. Regardless of the religious doctrine, some Catholic women

may not want to observe it. Catholic women get abortions at higher rates than the general population (Henshaw and Kost 1996).

2. The point of viability is debated. Some very early-gestation fetuses (circa twenty-three weeks) have survived, but with serious health impairments and disabilities. For an overview of the issue, see Krissi Danielsson, About.com, "Premature Birth and Viability," *miscarriage.about.com/od/pregnancyafterloss/a/prematurebirth.htm*, accessed November 23, 2009.

3. Perinatologists frequently receive referrals to do second-trimester pregnancy terminations for genetic or medical reasons. Dr. Smits would not have expected to do first-trimester terminations regardless of where he practiced because, as a specialist, for the most part he does not have patients with early unwanted pregnancies. Most of his patients want to be pregnant and may be having problems with the pregnancy. Pregnant women usually only find out about genetic and medical problems about sixteen to twenty weeks into the pregnancy, after amniocentesis (for more about this, see Rapp 1999), although this is changing slightly with the advances in earlier methods of genetic testing (for instance, a nuchal scan, to help identify Down syndrome, can be done at eleven to fourteen weeks).

4. I heard about such scenarios on my thirteenth and fifteenth interviews (out of forty), and after that point I started soliciting discussion on the topic from the remaining physicians I interviewed. Therefore, I do not know exactly what portion of the physicians in my study had such experiences.

5. The Catholic position on abortion is articulated in the following excerpts of the Catholic catechism: "Human life must be respected and protected absolutely from the moment of conception. From the first moment of his existence, a human being must be recognized as having the rights of a person . . . abortion and infanticide are abominable crimes." For more detail see, Priests for Life, "Excerpts from the Catechism of the Catholic Church on Life, Abortion and Euthanasia," *www.priestsforlife.org/magisterium/catechismonabortion.htm*, accessed November 17, 2009. The management of ectopic pregnancy (a fertilized ovum that implants in the fallopian tube, has no chance of survival, and threatens the life of the pregnant woman) brings up the same set of political and religious issues that are hotly debated among physicians and theologians. The debate revolves around whether medication (methotrexate) can be used to kill the growing embryo, which would spare the woman's fallopian tube for future use, or following stricter interpretation of Catholic doctrine, whether the entire fallopian tube should be removed so the physician indirectly kills the fetus. Assuming that the woman had two functioning tubes, she would lose 50 percent of her fertility in this process. I did not hear much about this in my interviews, so I do not address it here. For more information on the debate, see Dickens, Faundes, and Cook (2003) and Pivarunas (2003).

6. The Catholic Hospital Association became today's Catholic Health Association, both referred to by the abbreviation CHA.

7. Before this, a Catholic hospital policy toward abortion, titled "The Surgical Code for Catholic Hospitals," was written in 1921 by Rev. Michael Burke: "Operations *directly destructive* of life were prohibited, but . . . procedures *indirectly* harmful or destructive to the fetus were permitted" (italics in the original text) (Joyce 2002: 109). This was written largely to pacify Catholics who wanted a stricter codification of their law, but Moulinier deemphasized it, asserting that application of the codes was up to the individual hospitals (Joyce 2002: 110). The 1921 policy was written as a list of dos and don'ts (comparatively simpler than the pamphlet version produced later) and hung on operating room walls (O'Rourke, Kopfen-Steiner, and Hamel 2001).

8. David Solomon was trained in philosophy and works for the Center for Ethics and Culture at the University of Notre Dame. This definition, excerpted from Becker and Becker (2001), is available at *www.saintmarys.edu/~incandel/double effect.html*, "The Principle of Double Effect."

9. The term *threatened abortion* in this context refers to probable oncoming spontaneous abortion or miscarriage, where the body tries to expel the fetus, as opposed to *therapeutic* or *induced abortion*, which is brought about through surgical or medical intervention.

10. The Emergency Medical Treatment and Active Labor Act is a statute that governs when and how patients may be refused treatment or transferred from one hospital to another when they are in an unstable medical condition. It is a nondiscrimination statute that applies to nearly all hospitals in the United States to ensure that all patients presenting with an emergency condition are treated regardless of their ability to pay and that they are not transferred to "charity" or "county hospitals." For more information see U.S. Department of Health and Human Services, Centers for Medicare and Medicaid Services, EMTALA Overview, *www.cms.hhs.gov/EMTALA/*.

11. Disseminated intravascular coagulapathy (DIC) is a life-threatening complication of sepsis where the blood starts to coagulate throughout the body; often associated with hemorrhage.

12. Kathleen Joyce's article (2002) discusses the popular interest in Catholic health care generated by Paul Blanshard's book *American Freedom and Catholic Power* (1949), Edward J. Edwards's *Dark Enemy* (1954), and Henry Morton Robinson's *The Cardinal* (1950), which was made into a film by Otto Preminger in 1963.

Notes to Chapter 7

1. Obstetrics and gynecology is one of the most highly litigious areas of medicine, and physician lawsuits for bad birth outcomes can be very expensive. This legal pressure has had an effect on ob-gyn birth practices, creating protocols to protect the physician that critics argue are not best for the pregnant woman. These critiques, since the 1970s, have to some extent revived the practice of midwifery

in the United States, largely in the hospital setting, but home-birth midwifery is increasingly common as well.

2. See "Fellowship in Family Planning," *www.familyplanningfellowship.org/*, accessed May 24, 2008.

3. See the Kenneth J. Ryan Residency Training Program in Abortion and Family Planning, *www.ryanprogram.org/*, and the Bixby Center for Global Reproductive Health, *bixbycenter.ucsf.edu/training/training/kenneth_j_ryan_training .html*, both accessed November 20, 2009.

4. See the National Abortion Federation, "Timeline, State by State: Expanding CNM, NP, and PA Provision of Abortion Care," *www.prochoice.org/cfc/resources /timeline.html*, accessed November 20, 2009.

WORKS CITED

Abbott, A. 1983. "Professional ethics." *American Journal of Sociology* 88:855–85.

ACOG, American College of Obstetrics and Gynecology. 2007. *ACOG Committee Opinion No. 385:* "The limits of conscience refusal in reproductive medicine." *Obstetrics and Gynecology* 110(5):1203–8.

ACS, American College of Surgeons. 1993. *Socio-economic factbook for surgery.* Chicago: American College of Surgeons.

AJOG, *American Journal of Obstetrics and Gynecology.* 1972. "A statement on abortion by one hundred professors of obstetrics." *American Journal of Obstetrics and Gynecology* 112:992–98.

Almeling, R., L. Tews, and S. Dudley. 2000. "Abortion training in U.S. obstetrics and gynecology residency programs, 1998." *Family Planning Perspectives* 32:268–71, 320.

Anspach, R. R. 1993. *Deciding who lives: Fateful choices in the intensive-care nursery.* Berkeley: University of California Press.

Atwood, T. C. 2007. "Adoption factbook IV: The most comprehensive source for adoption statistics nationwide." Alexandria, VA: National Council for Adoption.

Becker, L. C., and C. B. Becker. 2001. *Encyclopedia of ethics.* New York: Routledge.

Bellandi, D. 1998. "Access declines. Reproductive services fall with hospital consolidation." *Modern Healthcare* 28:26.

Bosk, C. L. 1979. *Forgive and remember: Managing medical failure.* Chicago: University of Chicago Press.

———. 1992. *All God's mistakes: Genetic counseling in a pediatric hospital.* Chicago: University of Chicago Press.

———. 2006. "Review essay: Avoiding conventional understandings: The enduring legacy of Eliot Freidson." *Sociology of Health and Illness* 28:637–46.

Brahmi, D., C. Dehlendorf, D. Engel, K. Grumbach, C. Joffe, and M. Gold. 2007. "A descriptive analysis of abortion training in family medicine residency programs." *Family Medicine* 39:399–403.

Brooks, P. 2006. "Merge talk under way for Kingston's two hospitals." *Times Herald-Record,* November 30.

Burgoine, G. A., S. D. Van Kirk, J. Romm, A. B. Edelman, S. L. Jacobson, and J. T. Jensen. 2005. "Comparison of perinatal grief after dilation and evacuation or labor induction in second trimester terminations for fetal anomalies." *American Journal of Obstetrics and Gynecology* 192:1928–32.

Casalino, L. P., K. J. Devers, T. K. Lake, M. Reed, and J. J. Stoddard. 2003. "Benefits of and barriers to large medical group practice in the United States." *Archives of Internal Medicine* 163(16): 1958–64.

Casper, M. J. 1998. *The making of the unborn patient: A social anatomy of fetal surgery.* New Brunswick, NJ: Rutgers University Press.

CHA, Catholic Health Association. 2001. "Ethical and religious directives for Catholic health care services." *Origins* 31:153, 155–63; also at United States Conference of Catholic Bishops, *www.usccb.org/bishops/directives.shtml.*

———. 2009. "Catholic health care in the United States," *www.chausa.org/NR /rdonlyres/68B7C0E5-F9AA-4106-B182-7DF0FC30A1CA/0/FACTSHEET.pdf.*

Charo, R. A. 2005. "The celestial fire of conscience—refusing to deliver medical care." *New England Journal of Medicine* 352:2471–73.

———. 2007. "The partial death of abortion rights." *New England Journal of Medicine* 356:2125–28.

Chervenak, F. A., and L. B. McCullough. 2008. "The ethics of direct and indirect referral for termination of pregnancy." *American Journal of Obstetrics and Gynecology* 199:232 e1–3.

Clarke, A. 1998. *Disciplining reproduction modernity, American life sciences, and the problems of sex.* Berkeley: University of California Press.

Connolly, C. 2005. "Access to abortion pared at state level." *Washington Post,* August 29, A1, A4.

Conrad, P. 2006. "Eliot Freidson's revolution in medical sociology." *Health: An Interdisciplinary Journal for the Social Study of Health, Illness and Medicine* 11:141–44.

CRR, Center for Reproductive Rights. 2007. "Targeted regulation of abortion providers (TRAP): Avoiding the TRAP." New York, *www.reproductiverights.org/pub_fac_ trap.html.*

Curlin, F. A., R. E. Lawrence, M. H. Chin, and J. D. Lantos. 2007. "Religion, conscience, and controversial clinical practices." *New England Journal of Medicine* 356:593–600.

Darney, P. D., U. Landy, S. MacPherson, and R. L. Sweet. 1987. "Abortion training in U.S. obstetrics and gynecology residency programs." *Family Planning Perspectives* 19:158–62.

deBlois, J., and K. D. O'Rourke. 1995. "Care for the beginning of life: The revised Ethical and Religious Directives discuss abortion, contraception, and assisted reproduction." *Health Progress* 76:36–40.

DeFrances, C. J., and M. J. Hall. 2007. "2005 national hospital discharge survey." *Advance Data from Vital and Health Statistics* 385, July 12, *www.cdc.gov/nchs/data /ad/ad385.pdf.*

Dehlendorf, C., D. Brahmi, D. Engel, K. Grumbach, C. Joffe, and M. Gold. 2007. "Integrating abortion training into family medicine residency programs." *Family Medicine* 39:337–42.

Dickens, B. 2008. "Conscientious commitment." *Lancet* 371:1240–41.

Dickens, B. M., A. Faundes, and R. J. Cook. 2003. "Ectopic pregnancy and emergency care: Ethical and legal issues." *International Journal of Gynecology and Obstetrics* 82:121–26.

Donohoe, M. 2005. "Increase in obstacles to abortion: The American perspective in 2004." *Journal of the American Medical Women's Association* 60:16–25.

Eastwood, K. L., J. E. Kacmar, J. Steinauer, S. Weitzen, and L. A. Boardman. 2006. "Abortion training in United States obstetrics and gynecology residency programs." *Obstetrics and Gynecology* 108:303–8.

Epstein, S. 1996. *Impure science: AIDS, activism, and the politics of knowledge.* Berkeley: University of California Press.

Fawcus, S. R. 2008. "Maternal mortality and unsafe abortion." *Best Practice and Research Clinical Obstetrics and Gynaecology* 22(3):533–48.

Fernandez, M. M., F. Coeytaux, R. G. de Leon, and D. L. Harrison. 2009. "Assessing the global availability of misoprostol." *International Journal of Gynecology and Obstetrics* 105:180–6.

Fields, J. 2008. *Risky lessons: Sex education and social inequality.* New Brunswick, NJ: Rutgers University Press.

Fletcher, K. E., W. Underwood III, S. Q. Davis, R. S. Mangrulkar, L. F. McMahon Jr., and S. Saint. 2005. "Effects of work hour reduction on residents' lives: A systematic review." *Journal of the American Medical Association* 294:1088–1100.

Fogel, S. B., and L. A. Rivera. 2004. "Saving Roe is not enough: When religion controls healthcare." *Fordham Urban Law J* 31:725–49.

Forrest, J. D., C. Tietze, and E. Sullivan. 1978. "Abortion in the United States, 1976–1977." *Family Planning Perspectives* 10:271–79.

Foster, A. M., J. van Dis, and J. E. Steinauer. 2003. "Educational and legislative initiatives affecting residency training in abortion." *Journal of the American Medical Association* 290:1777–78.

Foucault, M. 1973. *The birth of the clinic: An archaeology of medical perception.* New York: Pantheon Books.

———. 1978. *The history of sexuality.* New York: Pantheon Books.

Fox, R. C. 1957. "Training for uncertainty." In *The student-physician: Introductory studies in the sociology of medical education,* edited by R. K. Merton, G. G. Reader, and P. L. Kendall, 207–41. Cambridge, MA: Harvard University Press.

Freidson, E. 1970. *Profession of medicine: A study of the sociology of applied knowledge.* New York: Dodd Mead.

———. 1984. "The changing nature of professional control." *Annual Review of Sociology* 10:1–20.

———. 1994. *Professionalism reborn: Theory, prophecy, and policy.* Chicago: University of Chicago Press.

Gallagher, J. 1997. "Religious freedom, reproductive health care, and hospital mergers." *Journal of the American Medical Women's Association* 52:65–68.

Gelb, J., and C. J. Shogan. 2005. "Community activism in the USA: Catholic hospital mergers and reproductive access." *Social Movement Studies* 4:209–29.

Gilligan, C. 1982. *In a different voice: Psychological theory and women's development.* Cambridge, MA: Harvard University Press.

Ginsburg, F. D. 1998. *Contested lives: The abortion debate in an American community.* Berkeley: University of California Press.

Goffman, E. 1963. *Stigma: Notes on the management of spoiled identity.* Englewood Cliffs, NJ: Prentice-Hall.

Gonzales v. Carhart. 2007. 127 S. Ct. 1610.

Greene, M. F. 2007. "The intimidation of American physicians: Banning partial-birth abortion." *New England Journal of Medicine* 356(21):2128–29.

Grimes, D. A. 2008. "The choice of second trimester abortion method: Evolution, evidence and ethics." *Reproductive Health Matters* 16:183–88.

Grimes, D. A., J. Benson, S. Singh, M. Romero, B. Ganatra, F. E. Okonofua, and I. H. Shah. 2006. "Unsafe abortion: The preventable pandemic." *Lancet* 368: 1908–19.

Grimes, D. A., and K. F. Schulz. 1985. "Morbidity and mortality from second-trimester abortions." *Journal of Reproductive Medicine* 30:505–14.

Guttmacher Institute. 2006. "Contraception counts: Ranking state efforts." *In Brief,* 2006 series, No. 1, *www.guttmacher.org/pubs/2006/02/28/IB2006n1.pdf.*

Hafferty, F. W., and D. W. Light. 1995. "Professional dynamics and the changing nature of medical work." *Journal of Health and Social Behavior* Spec No: 132–53.

Halfmann, D. 2003. "Historical priorities and the responses of doctors' associations to abortion reform proposals in Britain and the United States, 1960–1973." *Social Problems* 50:567–91.

Hammarstedt, M., A. Lalos, and M. Wulff. 2006. "A population-based study of Swedish gynecologists' experiences of working in abortion care." *Acta Obstetricia et Gynecologica Scandinavica* 85:229-35.

Harper, C. C., K. Blanchard, D. Grossman, J. T. Henderson, and P. D. Darney. 2007. "Reducing maternal mortality due to elective abortion: Potential impact of misoprostol in low-resource settings." *International Journal of Gynecology and Obstetrics* 98:66–9.

Harries, J., K. Stinson, and P. Orner. 2009. "Health care providers' attitudes towards termination of pregnancy: A qualitative study in South Africa." *BMC Public Health* 9:296.

Hartley, H. 2002. "The system of alignments challenging physician professional dominance: An elaborated theory of countervailing powers." *Sociology of Health and Illness* 24:178–207.

Haug, M. R. 1976. "The erosion of professional authority: A cross-cultural inquiry in the case of the physician." *Milbank Memorial Fund Quarterly Health and Society* 54:83–106.

———. 1988. "A re-examination of the hypothesis of physician deprofessionalization." *Milbank Quarterly* 66 Supplement 2:48–56.

Haug, M. R., and B. Lavin. 1978. "Method of payment for medical care and public attitudes toward physician authority." *Journal of Health and Social Behavior* 19:279–91.

Hayward, R. S., K. Rockwood, G. J. Sheehan, and E. B. Bass. 1991. "A phenomenology of scut." *Annals of Internal Medicine* 115:372–76.

Henshaw, S. K., and K. Kost. 1996. "Abortion patients in 1994–1995: Characteristics and contraceptive use." *Family Planning Perspectives* 28:140–47, 158.

Hochschild, A. R. 1985. *The managed heart: Commercialization of human feeling.* Berkeley: University of California Press.

Hodgson, J. E. 1995. "Violence versus reproductive health care." *BMJ* 310: 547–48.

Hughes, E. C., and L. A. Coser. 1994. *On work, race, and the sociological imagination.* Chicago: University of Chicago Press.

Hughes, P., and S. Riches. 2003. "Psychological aspects of perinatal loss." *Current Opinion in Obstetrics and Gynecology* 15:107–11.

Hunter, N. D. 2006. "Justice Blackmun, abortion, and the myth of medical independence." *Brooklyn Law Review* 72:147–97.

Imber, J. B. 1986. *Abortion and the private practice of medicine.* New Haven, CT: Yale University Press.

Jaffe, F. S., B. L. Lindheim, and P. R. Lee. 1981. *Abortion politics: Private morality and public policy.* New York: McGraw-Hill.

Jensen, J. T., S. M. Harvey, and L. J. Beckman. 2000. "Acceptability of suction curettage and mifepristone abortion in the United States: A prospective comparison study." *American Journal of Obstetrics and Gynecology* 182:1292–99.

Joffe, C. E. 1986. *The regulation of sexuality: Experiences of family planning workers.* Philadelphia: Temple University Press.

———. 1995. *Doctors of conscience: The struggle to provide abortion before and after* Roe v. Wade. Boston: Beacon Press.

———. 2010. *Dispatches from the abortion wars: The costs of fanaticism to doctors, patients, and the rest of us.* Boston: Beacon Press.

Joffe, C. E., P. Anderson, and J. E. Steinauer. 1998. "The crisis in abortion provision and pro-choice medical activism in the 1990s." In *Abortion wars: A half century of struggle, 1950–2000,* edited by Rickie Solinger, 320–33. Berkeley: University of California Press.

Joffe, C. E., and T. A. Weitz. 2003. "Normalizing the exceptional: Incorporating the 'abortion pill' into mainstream medicine." *Social Science and Medicine* 56:2353–66.

Jones, R. K., M. R. S. Zolna, S. K. Henshaw, and L. B. Finer. 2008. "Abortion in the United States: Incidence and access to services, 2005." *Perspectives on Sexual and Reproductive Health* 40:6–16.

Joyce, K. M. 2002. "The evil of abortion and the greater good of the faith: Negotiating Catholic survival in the twentieth-century American health care system." *Religion and American Culture* 12:91–121.

Kaltreider, N. B., S. Goldsmith, and A. J. Margolis. 1979. "The impact of midtrimester abortion techniques on patients and staff." *American Journal of Obstetrics and Gynecology* 135:235–38.

Kaufman, S. R. 2005. *And a time to die: How American hospitals shape the end of life.* New York: Scribner.

Kirk, E. P. 1984. "Psychological effects and management of perinatal loss." *American Journal of Obstetrics and Gynecology* 149:46–51.

Kletke, P. R., D. W. Emmons, and K. D. Gillis. 1996. "Current trends in physicians' practice arrangements: From owners to employees." *JAMA* 276:555–60.

Klingberg-Allvin, M., N. T. Nga, A. B. Ransjo-Arvidson, and A. Johansson. 2006. "Perspectives of midwives and doctors on adolescent sexuality and abortion care in Vietnam." *Scandinavian Journal of Public Health* 34:414–21.

Kummer, J. M., and Z. Leavy. 1966. "Therapeutic abortion law confusion." *JAMA* 195:96–100.

Labi, N. 1999. "Holy owned: Is it fair for a Catholic hospital to impose its morals on patients?" *Time* 154:85–86.

Lader, L. 1966. *Abortion.* Indianapolis: Bobbs-Merrill.

Landy, U. 2005. "Is family planning a subspecialty of obstetrics and gynecology?" *Contraception* 72:399–401.

Landy, U., and J. E. Steinauer. 2001. "How available is abortion training?" *Family Planning Perspectives* 33:88–89.

Liebhaber, A., and J. M. Grossman. 2007. "Physicians moving to mid-sized, single-specialty practices." *Tracking Report* 18:1–5.

Lief, H. I., and R. C. Fox. 1963. "Training for 'detached concern' in medical students." In *The psychological basis of medical practice*, edited by V. F. Lief, H. I. Lief, and R. C. Fox. New York: Harper and Row.

Lindheim, B. L. 1979. "Services, policies and costs in U.S. abortion facilities." *Family Planning Perspectives* 11:283–89.

Link, B. G., and J. C. Phelan. 2001. "Conceptualizing stigma." *Annual Review of Sociology* 27:363–85.

Linn, L. S., R. H. Brook, V. A. Clark, A. R. Davies, A. Fink, and J. Kosecoff. 1985. "Physician and patient satisfaction as factors related to the organization of internal medicine group practices." *Medical Care* 23:1171–78.

Lohr, P. A. 2008. "Surgical abortion in the second trimester." *Reproductive Health Matters* 16:151–61.

Luker, K. 1984. *Abortion and the politics of motherhood.* Berkeley: University of California Press.

——. 2006. *When sex goes to school: Warring views on sex—and sex education—since the sixties.* New York: W. W. Norton.

Lynch, H. F. 2008. *Conflicts of conscience in health care: An institutional compromise.* Cambridge, MA: MIT Press.

MacKay, H. T., and A. P. MacKay. 1995. "Abortion training in obstetrics and gynecology residency programs in the United States, 1991–1992." *Family Planning Perspectives* 27:112–15.

Madison, D. L., and T. R. Konrad. 1988. "Large medical group-practice organizations and employed physicians: A relationship in transition." *Milbank Quarterly* 66:240–82.

Marder, W. D., D. W. Emmons, P. R. Kletke, and R. J. Willke. 1988. "DataWatch. Physician employment patterns: Challenging conventional wisdom." *Health Affairs (Millwood)* 7:137–45.

Maslach, C. 1982. *Burnout: The cost of caring.* Englewood Cliffs, NJ: Prentice-Hall.

McKinlay, J. B., and L. D. Marceau. 2002. "The end of the golden age of doctoring." *International Journal Health Services* 32:379–416.

McKinlay, J. B., and J. D. Stoeckle. 1988. "Corporatization and the social transformation of doctoring." *International Journal Health Services* 18:191–205.

Mills, C. W. 1959. *The sociological imagination.* New York: Oxford University Press.

Mohr, J. C. 1978. *Abortion in America: The origins and evolution of national policy, 1800–1900.* New York: Oxford University Press.

Nader, L. 1969. "Up the anthropologist—Perspectives gained from studying up." In *Reinventing anthropology,* edited by D. Hymes, 284–311. New York: Random House.

O'Rourke, K. D., T. Kopfen-Steiner, and R. Hamel. 2001. "A brief history: A summary of the development of the Ethical and Religious Directives for Catholic Health Care Services." *Health Progress* 82:18–21.

Owings, M. F., and L. J. Kozak. 1998. "Ambulatory and inpatient procedures in the United States, 1996." *Vital Health Statistics* 13:1–119.

Palley, M. L., and T. Kohler. 2003. "Hospital mergers: The future of women's reproductive healthcare services." *Women and Politics* 25:149–78.

Parsons, T. 1951. *The social system.* Glencoe, IL: Free Press.

Pescosolido, B. A., S. A. Tuch, and J. K. Martin. 2001. "The profession of medicine and the public: Examining Americans' changing confidence in physician authority from the beginning of the 'health care crisis' to the era of health care reform." *Journal of Health and Social Behavior* 42:1–16.

Petchesky, R. P. 1990. *Abortion and woman's choice: The state, sexuality, and reproductive freedom.* Boston: Northeastern University Press.

Pivarunas, A. R. 2003. "Ethical and medical considerations in the treatment of ectopic pregnancy." *Linacre Quarterly* 70:195–209.

Place, M. D. 1998. "Toward a common vision for the Catholic health ministry." *Health Progress* 79:8–9, 16.

Rapp, R. 1999. *Testing women, testing the fetus: The social impact of amniocentesis in America*. New York: Routledge.

Reagan, L. J. 1997. *When abortion was a crime: Women, medicine, and law in the United States, 1867–1973*. Berkeley: University of California Press.

Reissman, C. K.. 1998. "Women and medicalization: A new perspective." In *The politics of women's bodies*, edited by Rose Weitz, 46–64. New York: Oxford University Press.

Richards, C. L. 2007. "The adoption vs. abortion myth." *Los Angeles Times*, October 29. Accessed at LATimes.com.

Rose, M. 2007. *Safe, legal, and unavailable?: Abortion politics in the United States*. Washington, DC: CQ Press.

Rose, N. 2001. "The politics of life itself." *Theory, Culture and Society* 18:1–30.

Rothman, D. J. 1991. *Strangers at the bedside: A history of how law and bioethics transformed medical decision making*. New York: Basic Books.

Ruzek, S. B. 1978. *The women's health movement: Feminist alternatives to medical control*. New York: Praeger.

Schwarz, R. H. 1968. "Endotoxin shock in abortion: Current concepts." *Medical Times* 96:65–69.

Shochet, T., and J. Trussell. 2008. "Determinants of demand: Method selection and provider preference among US women seeking abortion services." *Contraception* 77:397–404.

Simonds, W. 1996. *Abortion at work: Ideology and practice in a feminist clinic*. New Brunswick, NJ: Rutgers University Press.

Sloboda, M. 2001. "The high cost of merging with a religiously-controlled hospital." *Berkeley Women's Law Journal* 16:140–56.

Smith, A., and S. Kleinman. 1989. "Managing emotions in medical school: Students' contacts with the living and the dead." *Social Psychology Quarterly* 52:56–59.

Smith-Rosenberg, C. 1986. *Disorderly conduct: Visions of gender in Victorian America*. New York: Oxford University Press.

Sorrell, A. L. 2009. "Ending abortion conscience rule?" In *American Medical News*, March 23, *www.ama-assn.org/amednews/2009/03/23/gvsa0323.htm*.

Spillar, K. 2009. "Crisis of deception: Fake clinics spread misinformation on the federal dime." RH Reality Check, July 8, *www.rhrealitycheck.org/blog/2009/07/08/crisis-deception-fake-clinics-spread-misinformation-federal-dime*.

Starr, P. 1982. *The social transformation of American medicine*. New York: Basic Books.

Steinauer, J. E., U. Landy, H. Filippone, D. Laube, P. D. Darney, and R. A. Jackson. 2008. "Predictors of abortion provision among practicing obstetrician-gynecologists: A national survey." *American Journal of Obstetrics and Gynecology* 198:39 e1–6.

Steinauer, J. E., U. Landy, R. A. Jackson, and P. D. Darney. 2003. "The effect of training on the provision of elective abortion: A survey of five residency programs." *American Journal of Obstetrics and Gynecology* 188:1161–63.

Steinauer, J. E., M. Silveira, R. Lewis, F. Preskill, and U. Landy. 2007. "Impact of formal family planning residency training on clinical competence in uterine evacuation techniques." *Contraception* 76:372–76.

Strauss, L. T., S. B. Gamble, W. Y. Parker, D. A. Cook, S. B. Zane, and S. Hamdan. 2006. "Abortion surveillance—United States, 2003." *Morbidity and Mortality Weekly Report Surveillance Summary* 55:1–32.

Strauss, L. T., J. Herndon, J. Chang, W. Y. Parker, D. A. Levy, S. B. Bowens, S. B. Zane, and C. J. Berg. 2004. "Abortion surveillance—United States, 2001." *Morbidity and Mortality Weekly Report Surveillance Summary* 53:1–32.

Sullivan, D. A., and R. Weitz. 1988. *Labor pains: Modern midwives and home birth.* New Haven, CT: Yale University Press.

Tietze, C. 1980. *Induced abortion: 1979.* New York: Population Council.

Timmermans, S. 1999. *Sudden death and the myth of CPR.* Philadelphia: Temple University Press.

Timmermans, S., and M. Berg. 2003. *The gold standard: The challenge of evidence-based medicine and standardization in health care.* Philadelphia: Temple University Press.

U.S. Bureau of Labor Statistics, U.S. Department of Labor. 2008. "Women in the labor force: A databook." Report 1011, *www.bls.gov/cps/wlf-databook2008.htm.*

Uttley, L., and R. Pawelko. 2002. *No strings attached: Public funding of religiously sponsored hospitals in the United States.* Albany, NY: Education Fund of Family Planning Advocates of New York State, *www.mergerwatch.org/pdfs/bp_no_strings.pdf.*

Ventura, S. J., W. D. Mosher, S. C. Curtin, J. C. Abma, and S. Henshaw. 2000. "Trends in pregnancies and pregnancy rates by outcome: Estimates for the United States, 1976–96." *Vital Health Statistics* 21:1–47.

Vitello, P. 2006. "Used to big losses, Schenectady is hit hard by plan for hospitals." *New York Times*, December 4.

Warenius, L. U., E. A. Faxelid, P. N. Chishimba, J. O. Musandu, A. A. Ong'any, and E. B. Nissen. 2006. "Nurse-midwives' attitudes towards adolescent sexual and reproductive health needs in Kenya and Zambia." *Reproductive Health Matters* 14:119–28.

Warren, M. G., R. Weitz, and S. Kulis. 1998. "Physician satisfaction in a changing health care environment: The impact of challenges to professional autonomy, authority, and dominance." *Journal of Health and Social Behavior* 39:356–67.

Weitz, T. A., P. Anderson, and D. Taylor. 2009. "Advancing scope of practice for advanced practice clinicians: More than a matter of access." *Contraception* 80:105–7.

Weitz, T. A., and S. Yanow. 2008. "Implications of the federal abortion ban for women's health in the United States." *Reproductive Health Matters* 16:99–107.

Wicklund, S., and A. S. Kesselheim. 2007. *This common secret: My journey as an abortion doctor.* New York: Public Affairs.

Yardley, J., and D. Rohde. 1998. "Abortion doctor in Buffalo slain; sniper attack fits violent pattern." *New York Times,* October 25, A1.

Zussman, R. 1992. *Intensive care: Medical ethics and the medical profession.* Chicago: University of Chicago Press.

INDEX

abortion
 as birth control, 42–43
 Catholic position on, 122–23, 170n5,
  171n7
 complications associated with, 72
 cost of, 28
 criminalization of, 10–11, 31, 139, 146–47
 deaths from, 12–13
 elective, 2, 159–60n3
 emotional aspects of, 46–47, 68–69, 70,
  76–82, 165n2
 history of, 3–4, 9–13, 21–22, 139–40
 incidence of, 3, 160n4
 and maternal health exemption in
  Catholic doctrine, 122–27
 medication, 35, 101–2, 152, 164n15,
  169n4
 as moral issue, 8–9, 41–47, 58–59, 76–82,
  145–47
 as outpatient procedure, 23
 political dimensions of, 7–9, 49–50
 public health narrative of, 81–82
 referrals for, 68–69, 104–5, 142
 in the second trimester, 73–75, 77–79,
  80–81, 82–86, 100–101, 105–6, 107,
  169n6
 segregation of from mainstream
  medicine, 2–3, 20–30
 terminology for, 160n3
 therapeutic, 12, 171n9
 See also miscarriage; Roe v. Wade
abortion, illegal, 92
 risks of, 2, 12–13, 146–47
 tolerance of, 11–12

Abortion Access Project, 162–63n10
abortion care
 advocates for integration of, 20, 27–28,
  91–92, 139–40
 consequences of marginalization of,
  25–30, 36
 ethics of, 78–79
 future of, 149–52
 after Roe v. Wade, 22–25
 in rural areas, 34, 35, 111
 standards for, 23–24, 30–31
 in the U.S. versus other countries, 149
 See also abortion providers
abortion clinics
 freestanding, 3, 4, 20, 21–22, 23, 25,
  111–16, 117, 147
 See also abortion providers
abortionist (as problematic label), 92–93, 116
abortion methods. See dilation and curettage;
  dilation and evacuation; dilation and
  extraction; labor induction; medication
  abortion
abortion patients
 empathy for, 70, 78–81, 90, 142
 misconceptions about, 67–68
 See also abortion care
abortion practice
 cultural and social constraints on, 15–16,
  24–25, 37–38, 52–54, 58–59, 70,
  92–97, 104–10, 138–39, 145, 152
 impact of managed care on, 28, 29, 36,
  113–14
 integration of into ob-gyn practice, 20,
  27–28, 54–57, 91–92, 115–16, 148–49

183